DATE DUE	
	RECEIVED FEB 9 1998	
	By	

A
Sure
Thing?

```
          NATIONAL  LEAGUE - SATURDAY, JU
BET#  TEAM         PITCHER        LINE    123
EVEN  PHILLIES     QUANTRILL              132
-110  CARDS        K HILL                 010
903   PIRATES      ERICKS        +165     8.5
904   EXPOS        C PEREZ       -175
905   MARLINS      HAMMOND       +143     8.5
906   REDS         SCHOUREK      -153
907   METS         MLICKI        +170     8.5
908   BRAVES       SMOLTZ        -180
909   CUBS         FOSTER        +129     8.5
910   ASTROS       KILE          -139
911   GIANTS       M LEITER      +172     7.5
912   DODGERS      NOMO          -182
913   ROCKIES      RITZ          +133     8
914   PADRES       HAMILTON      -143
          AMERICAN  LEAGUE - SATURDAY,
BET#  TEAM         PITCHER        LINE    12
+144  BLUE JAYS    JU GUZMAN               0
-154  YANKEES      M PEREZ                 00
917   RED SOX      WAKEFIELD     -130      9
918   ORIOLES      KLINGENBEC    +120
919   INDIANS      BLACK         -110      9
920   WHITE SOX    A FERNANDE    EVEN
921   BREWERS      GIVENS        +110     10
922   TIGERS       MOORE         -120
923   TWINS        ERICKSON      +145      8
924   ROYALS       GUBICZA       -155
925   A'S          DARLING       +135     10
926   RANGERS      PAVLIK        -145
927   ANGELS       FINLEY        +135
```

A
Sure
Thing?

SPORTS
—and—
GAMBLING

J E F F S A V A G E

To Todd Jarrett for not losing his shirt

The Publisher thanks Jay Coakley, Ph.D., Professor of Sociology at the University of Colorado, Colorado Springs, Colorado; Gary Funk, Director of Teacher Education and Graduate Studies at Southwestern College, Winfield, Kansas; and James H. Frey, Professor of Sociology at the University of Nevada, Las Vegas, for their assistance.

Library of Congress Cataloging-in-Publication Data

Savage, Jeff, 1961–
   A sure thing? : sports and gambling / Jeff Savage.
     p. cm.
   Includes bibliographical references and index.
   Summary: Discusses the ever-increasing gambling phenomenon of sports betting and the issues involved with it, such as societal and individual risks and benefits.
   ISBN 0–8225–3303–0 (alk. paper)
    1. Sports betting—United States—Juvenile literature.
2. Gambling—United States—Juvenile literature. [1. Sports betting. 2. Gambling .] I. Title.
GV717.S38 1997
796—dc20   96–25629

Manufactured in the United States of America
1 2 3 4 5 6 – JR – 02 01 00 99 98 97

CONTENTS

San Diego quarterback Stan Humphries fires off a pass during the 1995 Super Bowl.

CHAPTER ONE

PLAYING THE GAME

▪

One minute remains in the 1995 Super Bowl. The San Francisco 49ers lead the San Diego Chargers, 49–26. The outcome has been decided. The *action* has not. Todd Jarrett, a 33-year-old lifelong Chargers fan who flew in from San Diego and paid $250 for a ticket, is pressed up against the railing at Miami's Joe Robbie Stadium, screaming for San Francisco. Why? Jarrett has placed a bet on the 49ers. If the 49ers win by fewer than 20 points, he loses. "I love the Chargers, but I figured they would get blown out," Jarrett says. "So I bet $1,000 against them."

The Chargers are passing on every down. Wide receiver Tony Martin catches a pass over the middle and is tackled at San Francisco's 44-yard line. The Chargers hurry to the line as the clock ticks down . . . 55 seconds left, 54, 53 . . . Jarrett has a lump in his throat, and he's not the only one. ABC-TV announcer Al Michaels says, "A few people around this great land of ours have just moved to the forward portion of the couch." Commentator Dan Dierdorf laughs knowingly.

In the dying moments of the game, the Chargers are trailing by

23 points. Running back Ronnie Harmon reaches the 49ers' 35-yard line with a catch and the Chargers quickly call timeout. Ten seconds remain—enough time for two plays. Billions of dollars are riding on the finish, including $1,000 for Todd Jarrett, who can barely stand up.

Chargers quarterback Stan Humphries takes the snap, rolls right, and looks toward the end zone. "Hearts are beating fast all over the land," television announcer Michaels says, "as Humphries throws . . . incomplete." With two seconds left, Humphries throws again—a desperation pass that Deion Sanders intercepts in the end zone. It's over. The 49ers win the game by enough points for Todd Jarrett and millions of people like him to win their bets. Of course, the millions who bet on the Chargers lose.

Sports betting is a booming industry, mixing people's love for sports with their passion for gambling. In 1974, $50 million was bet legally on sports in Nevada. In 1990, 16 years later, that figure was $1.9 billion—nearly 40 times as much.[1] Gambling is legal where it is permitted by the state and where the government licenses, regulates, and taxes the people who participate in the betting. However, legal sports betting in gambling establishments, called casinos, and at racetracks doesn't begin to tell the story.

Illegal sports betting is a vast business involving millions of people and tens of billions of dollars each year. At least $60 billion is wagered illegally every year, according to the Federal Bureau of Investigation (FBI). "That figure is probably low," says Tom French, an FBI senior supervisor in New York.[2] Indeed, some estimates run as high as $100 billion a year. The Super Bowl is the ultimate betting event for the public, with an estimated $3 billion wagered on the game.[3] As noted sportswriter Frank Deford says, "Americans buy bets on the Super Bowl shamelessly, in the same holiday spirit as they purchase turkey at Thanksgiving or roses on Valentine's Day."[4]

Sports betting is just part of a gambling phenomenon in the United States. A national study in 1974 showed that 61 percent of the U.S. population gambled. A Gallup poll in 1989 raised that figure to 81 percent. Estimates in the 1990s ranged up to 88 percent.[5] People everywhere are playing the lottery by buying a ticket in a drawing for large amounts of money.

People gather in huge bingo halls to play for a chance at winning money.

Thousands play bingo in church basements, or card games and slot machines at casinos. More and more people are buying raffle tickets and playing games at carnivals and state fairs. They are wagering money in an attempt to acquire more money. And they are betting in ever-increasing numbers.

In 1974, Americans bet about $17 billion. In 1994, Americans bet $482 billion—legally.[6] Forty-eight states have some form of legalized gambling: casinos, horse racing, lotteries, raffles, or bingo.

(Hawaii and Utah are the exceptions.) Congress passed the Indian Gambling Regulatory Act in 1988, allowing Native Americans to operate casinos on their land. A year later, states began allowing gambling on riverboats.

In 1995, there were 37 state lotteries. Some 44 states offered wagering on horse and greyhound races. A gambler could play bingo in 47 states.[7] In 1996, Massachusetts and North Carolina became the 24th and 25th states to offer legal casino gambling to the public.

GAMBLING TERMS

Roulette is a game of chance that doesn't involve any skill. A small ball is tossed onto a revolving wheel that has numbered compartments. Players bet on which hole the ball will land in.

bet: To risk something of value, usually money, on an uncertain outcome. A bet is the amount of money put at risk. Other terms that mean the same thing are *gamble* and *wager*.

bookmaker: A person who takes bets on sporting events at fixed odds. Often shortened to *bookie.*

carryover: The amount of money a gambler owes to or is owed by a bookie before the account is settled.

casino: A building or room used for playing gambling games.

commercial gambling: Games of unequal chance, from which the operator of the game will make money over time. For example, a casino is able to remain in business because it pays winners less money, per bet, than it receives from losers. A state lottery or racetrack keeps a percentage of the money bet before it divides the remaining money between the winners. In contrast, in noncommercial gambling, such as when two people bet $1 on a coin toss, each person has an equal chance of winning the other's $1. If they bet a second time, each person again has an equal chance of winning $1.

compulsive gambler: A gambler who is unable to stop gambling, even when the results are unpleasant. Also called a *problem* gambler.

fix: To make a certain outcome happen by illegal methods, usually by paying someone who can determine the result.

illegal gambling: Gambling in a place or with people who are not licensed by the government.

legal gambling: Gambling that is licensed, regulated, and taxed by the government.

lottery: A game of chance that does not involve any skill. Players buy tickets. If a player's ticket is drawn, that player wins money or a prize. Also called a *raffle.*

money line: The betting odds a bookmaker or oddsmaker gives on a game or sports event.

odds: True odds are the probability of one thing happening rather than another. If an event is impossible, it has a probability of 0. If an event is certain to happen, it has a probability of 1. Every other probability is expressed as a fraction between 0 and 1. For example, if a coin is flipped, the probability of it landing with the heads side up is 1/2. That is, 1

out of every 2 flips, the heads side will land up. Each flip has the same odds because each flip is independent of every other flip. That means that even if the heads side has landed up for 25 consecutive flips, the odds of heads landing up on the 26th flip are still 1 out of 2.

Gamblers state the odds as the chances against an event's happening. If a six-sided die is rolled, the probability of any one side landing up is 1 out of 6, or 1/6. But gamblers say that the odds of that side landing up are 5 to 1. That means that there are five chances that some other side will land up and just one chance that the specific side will. The true odds are the odds of winning. The betting odds are the odds paid. If a gambler bets $5 to another gambler's $1 on a roll of the die, the betting odds are the same as the true odds. But betting odds are almost never true odds.

In gambling games of chance, such as a lottery or roulette, the mathematical odds can be calculated. The odds of the ball landing in any one hole of the roulette wheel are 38 to 1. But casinos pay a winner at roulette at 35 to 1 odds in order to ensure a profit for the casino. That is, a winning gambler gets $35 for every $1, not $38.

In gambling games of skill and chance, such as sports events, there is no mathematical way to calculate the probability of a specific outcome. Instead, gamblers base their opinions on previous performances, the weather, injuries, and other information. As commercial gamblers, casino operators and bookies use odds that will attract even amounts of betting on all possible outcomes. They pay off the winners at lower odds than the losers pay them to make money over the long term.

oddsmaker: A person who determines the betting odds of an event. Also called a *handicapper.*

pari-mutuel: A form of gambling in which the gamblers' bets determine how much money is won. The winning gamblers split the pool of money after the operator takes a percentage. Horse racing is the most common type of pari-mutuel gambling.

payoff odds: The betting odds. That is, the odds at which the bet is paid, not necessarily the true odds of an event occuring.

pick: The team on which a gambler chooses to bet.

point spread: Points a bookie adds to a team's score in order to get equal money bet on both teams in a game. Also called *spread, line, price,* and *number.*

point-shaving: Deliberately keeping the score of a game low in order to win a bet.

pool: The total amount of money at stake, usually the sum of the money bet by participants. Also called the *pot.*

professional gambler: A person who makes a living by gambling.

social gambler: A gambler who bets occasionally, usually as part of an accompanying social event. For example, a person who buys a chance in a tournament pool or bets on the Super Bowl.

sports book: A person who takes sports bets, or a place where those bets can be made.

vigorish: A fee charged for taking a bet. The fee can be obvious or it can be hidden in the mechanics of the game or the determination of the payoff odds. Also called *juice.*

The phenomenal increase in gambling reflects the growing acceptance of gambling as a legitimate form of relaxation. Once, most gambling was outlawed. Religious, civic, and political leaders told people that gambling was "bad" or "immoral" because it meant someone could get something without working for it. That attitude has changed.

In March 1995, California Senator Dianne Feinstein bet with Montana Senator Max Baucus on a women's college basketball game. Baucus bet $100 worth of Montana T-bone steaks that the Montana Lady Grizzlies would defeat San Diego State. Feinstein wagered a case of California red wine on the Aztecs. (For the record, Baucus and the Grizzlies won.) When government leaders make "friendly" wagers on sporting events, what kind of message do they send to the rest of America?

Religious groups often use bingo parties or ticket raffles to raise money for their social causes. Schools sponsor "casino nights" or carnivals to finance field trips and buy sports uniforms. States use money from lotteries to finance education and other public works. Some politicians like using gambling games, which people voluntarily choose to play, to raise money for government programs, rather than raising taxes, which everyone must pay. States advertise their lotteries and promote the idea of doing one's civic duty by buying lottery tickets. Some cities and states have tried to avoid bankruptcy by sponsoring lotteries and taxing gambling operations. However, as more and more gambling opportunities are offered, individual communities get smaller and smaller returns.

BETTING RISKS

Not everyone applauds the increase in gambling. Along with the increase in gamblers, researchers and sociologists have noted an increase in the number of people who are addicted to gambling. Henry Lesieur, a sociologist and researcher of gambling issues, says that between 4 and 6 percent of America's gamblers are problem, or compulsive, gamblers.[8] Valerie Lorenz at the National Center for Pathological Gambling in Baltimore, Maryland, agrees. She says, "We used to say, 'Work hard, study hard, and you'll get ahead.' Now we say, 'Just gamble. . . . Go for the big win.'"[9]

A whole new generation is betting like never before. A 1991 study of betting among college students, conducted by Lesieur, found that 23 percent gambled at least once a week.[10] "Anybody that doubts whether racing can attract a younger crowd," says Hollywood Park racetrack vice president Rick Baedeker, "ought to come here on a Friday and take a look at the crowd."[11]

STARTING YOUNG

Lesieur concluded in a 1987 study that 86 percent of New Jersey high school students had gambled within the previous year and 32 percent gambled at least once a week, mostly on sports events. "At first I didn't believe the rates," Lesieur said. "We double-checked and found that, if anything, we were conservative."[12] Another study, conducted in 1989 by Loma Linda University psychologist Durand Jacobs, surveyed 2,700 high school students in Connecticut, California, Virginia, and New Jersey. Jacobs's study showed that about half of those surveyed gambled at least once a year and about 5 percent gambled enough to be classified as problem gamblers.[13] When Lesieur did another

State lotteries attract casual bettors, who often don't think of themselves as "gamblers."

study in 1995, this time of more than 7,000 teenagers in the United States and Canada, he found that between 10 and 14 percent of those surveyed were at risk for developing gambling problems.[14] Although many groups are concerned about underage gambling, most research funds and efforts have been directed toward studying other social issues, such as teenage pregnancy, crack cocaine use, and AIDS awareness.

The estimated 7 to 11 percent of teenagers who are compulsive gamblers is a figure that almost all agree will continue to grow. Researchers in 1991 concluded that 1 million of the 8 million compulsive gamblers in the United States are teenagers.[15] Says Lesieur, "What you have now is a group of individuals who have no recollection of the time when gambling was outlawed. Gambling is simply around now. It's closer than ever before, and it's continuing to get closer."[16] Roger Svendsen, director of the Minnesota Compulsive Gambling Hotline, which serves a

Joseph Bail's painting, entitled *The Young Card Players*, illustrates that the issue of young gamblers is not a new one.

state where gambling has sky-rocketed since Native Americans opened casinos in 1989, says gambling is seen by most people as nothing more than an innocent hobby. "We're working with the first generation that has been raised when gambling has been seen as a positive thing," Svendsen says. "Instead of talking about gambling, we talk about *gaming*."[17]

A GAMBLING SPECIES

Gambling has existed throughout history. Cave dwellers during the Stone Age rolled dice made from shells or bones. Archaeologists surmise that the winners ate freshly killed meat and the losers starved. Archaeologists have found ancient Egyptians buried in the pyramids holding their loaded dice. (Loaded dice are heavier on one side, so the outcome of a toss is predictable.) Chinese warlords gambled away empires, and, according to the records of Chinese philosopher Confucius, the right arm of losing bettors was cut off and given to the winners. In Africa, men gambled away wives, children, and personal freedom. Men in India wagered on chariot racing. In ancient times, Greeks rolled oblong dice with rounded

This vase, which dates from the sixth century B.C., shows mythological Greek characters Ajax and Achilles playing a gambling game called draughts.

ends that were made from the an-klebones of sheep and Hebrews bet on pigeon racing. Augustus Caesar, a Roman emperor in the first century, ran the first recorded public lottery to make money for repairing Rome's roads. Romans also rolled dice and bet on chariot races and boxing matches.

The gambling history of North America begins with Native American games. Many native tribes had gambling games, but they apparently avoided some of the negative side effects by strictly regulating who could play the games and how much a person could lose.[18] Europeans brought gambling games with them to the New World. By 1638, the Puritans had passed the first antigambling law.[19] America's first president, George Washington, bet on cock-fights and horse races but tried to keep his soldiers from losing too much in their military camps.

Early nineteenth century bookmaking is depicted in this drawing by Charles Broughton.

Riverboat gamblers on Mississippi River vessels were notorious for cheating.

After winning their independence from England, Americans continued to gamble. They bought tickets in state lotteries and played card games in the California gold mining camps and on riverboats. By the 1800s, nearly every state had a lottery. By the 1870s, every state but Louisiana had outlawed them because of corruption. Lotteries were banned, nationwide, in 1893. Illegal gambling became the most lucrative moneymaking operation for criminal groups, such as the Mafia, after the law prohibiting the sale of alcohol was repealed. When Nevada legalized gambling in 1931, casinos quickly popped up and Mafia criminals controlled many of them. As the casino business became profitable and law enforcement officials cracked down on the Mafia and other organized crime groups, legitimate companies took over the gambling business in Las Vegas. New Hampshire changed its anti-lottery law and began a state lottery in 1963. In 1978, Atlantic City, New Jersey, became the eastern gathering place for gamblers. The decade of the 1980s was a boom time for legal gambling. Casinos, slot machines, riverboats, and state lotteries sprouted up in nearly every state. Those who wanted to encourage gambling opportunities began using the term "gaming" instead of gambling to present a friendlier, fun-loving image instead of the 1930s image of a gambler as a disreputable gangster.

"Gambling has been part of every known society," says Dr. Eric Plaut, a psychiatrist at Northwestern University Medical School. "What has changed in the past decade is that it is now publicly endorsed. The government is into the business of being an operator of gambling."[20]

The United States has become a nation of hungry bettors. Illegal gambling is hardly considered a crime anymore. Federal agents and local police officers have more pressing work. Author James Reston Jr. discusses this issue in his book *Collision at Home Plate*.

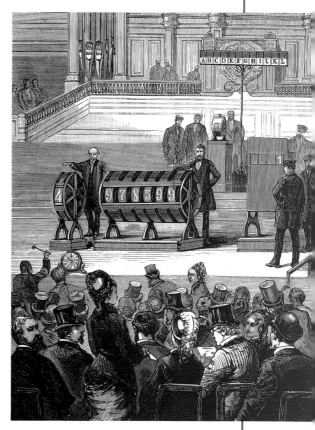

This drawing illustrates the popularity of an early lottery in France.

HORSE AND DOG RACING

Horse racing is a sport based on the speed of horses and the skill of jockeys. Horses race around an oval track to the finish line. Greyhound dog racing is similar except there are no jockeys. Instead, the dogs chase a mechanical lure that may resemble a bone or a rabbit or another greyhound. In 1996, there were 69 thoroughbred horse racing tracks in the United States and more than 60 dog tracks. More than 42 million people attended horse races in 1995.

The first recorded horse races were in about 1,500 B.C. when chariot races were held in eastern Europe and northern Africa. The Olympic Games in ancient Greece featured chariot racing in 680 B.C. Horse racing became known as the Sport of Kings because members of royalty in England owned racehorses and bet on races. Horse racing came to North America in the 1600s. Greyhound racing evolved from an ancient sport called "coursing" in which dogs chased a live rabbit across a field.

Spectators at horse and dog races can bet on the outcome of the races. Tracks use the *pari-mutuel system* of betting. All the money that is bet is combined into a fund called a pool or take. The odds of winning

are determined by the amount of money wagered on each horse (or dog) in proportion to the total money in the pool. The track takes a percentage of the money in each pool, usually about 17 percent, to make its profit and pay taxes. A certain percentage, called the *purse,* goes

Horse racing dates back thousands of years, and it is still a popular spectator sport.

to the horse owner. The remaining money is divided among the bettors. The favorite is the horse with the most money wagered on it. The odds on a favorite might be 2-to-1. If the favorite wins, a bettor who bet on that animal is paid $2 for every $1 bet. A long shot is a horse on which little money is bet. A long shot might have 30-to-1 odds. If the long shot wins, payment is $30 for every $1.

Bettors can also wager on an animal to place (finish second) or show (finish third). After odds are calculated, money collected in separate pools is paid to the winners.

"Historically, gambling has been downgraded in the [FBI's] priorities since the Nixon presidency."[21] President Bill Clinton, when asked about gambling in 1995, said simply, "Gambling is not a priority in this administration." After gambling prevention organizations called the White House to complain, Clinton said two days later that his administration was "looking at the gambling laws to see if they should be restructured."[22] Although many in government and law enforcement prefer to direct resources toward combating violent crime, pressure from some religious-right groups caused the House Judiciary Committee to approve a bill to create a nine-member National Gambling Impact and Policy Commission. The Commission will study the impact of legal gambling in the United States.

Sports betting is legal in five states, although only Nevada allows gamblers to bet on individual sports events. The other states—Delaware, Montana, Oregon, and North Dakota—offer sports betting through lottery games. Sports betting is so popular and goes on so openly, even where it is illegal, that virtually all major newspapers print the betting information on games. Television "experts" offer advice on which teams to pick, and *CNN Headline News* runs a sports ticker of up-to-the-minute scores to which tens of thousands of bettors keep tuned. What once was a back-alley operation handled mostly by organized crime has become a wide-open business.

HIGH-TECH BETS

Two developments have fueled the surge in sports betting: computers and television. Computers provide immediate information on odds, injuries, weather, and endless statistics that bettors use to make their wagers. "The amount of information available today is incredible," says Lem Banker, a professional gambler.[23]

Computer experts are busy designing software to place sports betting on the Internet, making it available to every American with a computer. Cyberspace casinos would not only give bettors access to more information, but they would also allow bettors to use credit cards to place their bets. Federal laws prohibit people in the gambling business from transmitting by wire any wager "in interstate or foreign commerce." But Sports International Ltd., a sports-betting house based in St. Johns, Antigua, has designed Virtual On-line Casino, and hopes to skirt U.S. gambling laws because it is not on U.S. soil. Wager-Net, another sports betting company that plans to operate from Belize, also expects a legal battle with the federal government. Kerry Rogers, a computer expert who designed WagerNet, is hopeful. "Imagine the millions of dollars bet worldwide on the World Cup," he says.[24]

Television—network and cable—has already brought more and more games into people's living rooms. For many viewers, the big question is not "What's the score?" but "What are the odds?" Horse racing was once the most popular sport for bettors. However, a study showed 40 percent of betting money in the 1980s went on football games, 32 percent on basketball games, and 21 percent on baseball games—all sports often shown on television.[25]

New York Police Department Deputy Chief Frank Biehler told *Forbes* magazine editor James Cook that he thinks sports betting will explode because of television. "Over the next two decades," says Biehler, "we will be able to wager

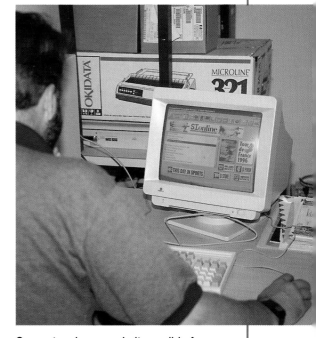

Computers have made it possible for gamblers to find information on gambling, and even opportunities to gamble, in their own homes and offices.

Television, especially with the creation of specialty cable channels, has boosted spectator interest in many sporting events.

through our cable television company—not only on the games but on halftime, the next play, the next hit, because we will have the technology."[26]

While illegal sports betting is accepted by the general public and often ignored by law enforcement officials, an important faction remains opposed to legalizing sports betting—the sports leagues themselves. Administrators of the leagues fear that as betting on sporting events increases, so will the risk of *fixing*—that is, gamblers paying athletes to deliberately lose and then betting against the athletes' team. Such corruption has happened before. League commissioners wish to preserve the public's trust that games are legitimate, not fixed.

The National Football League (NFL) protested in 1989 when Oregon introduced a football-betting lottery based on weekly NFL games. But Oregon legislators, who voted unanimously, were simply responding to polls that showed almost half of all westerners and northeasterners were ready to legalize betting on team sports. In fact, many believe that sports betting should be legal so it can be taxed. Revenues could be used to build parks and libraries or to reduce the national deficit. Proponents also point out that the NFL owes much of its commercial success to betting and the media publicity it receives. Indeed, some experts claim, the health of sports depends on betting. Without it, they say, interest in sports would deteriorate and there would be no more games.

Las Vegas casino manager Art Manteris predicts in his book, *SuperBookie,* that NFL stadiums will someday have wagering windows, just like horse racetracks. "It's absolutely conceivable to me," says Manteris, "that one day you will be able to wager at an NFL game."[27]

Jim Wimsatt, director of the New Hampshire Sweepstakes lottery, agrees with Manteris. "As soon as any state sports gambling operation volunteers to share revenue with the leagues," says Wimsatt, "it will not only be accepted, it will be blessed. Professional sports leagues simply want a piece of the pie."[28] Could such a scenario happen? Most gambling experts say it is likely.

How extensively will sports betting and other forms of gambling weave their way into the social fabric of America in the twenty-first century? Will the nation's children and young adults halt the rising tide of betting enthusiasm? Or is the United States on the brink of a national epidemic? William Jahoda ran a $20 million-a-year sports-betting operation in Chicago for a decade before he testified against the Mafia. He gives a dreary forecast. Jahoda says simply, "Betting will wreck this generation."[29]

CHAPTER TWO

WHERE THE ACTION IS

■

On March 19, 1931, the Nevada state government voted to legalize gambling. At the time, the 20-year-old town of Las Vegas was just a small cluster of ramshackle homes and card rooms in a vast, barren desert. With the legalization of gambling, casinos began to rise up from the desert floor. At the same time, Nevada made getting a divorce easier. People everywhere began flocking to the arid state to end marriages, and stayed to try their luck at gambling. Forty years later, Phil Tobin, the legislator who introduced the gambling bill, said that "Nevada would be a place today where people hurry through if the bill had not been passed."[1] Instead, Las Vegas is a booming city of nearly one million people. The Vegas Strip is a bustling three-mile stretch of towering casinos and blinking lights. Hordes of people scurry beneath the neon flashes to gamble the night away. Some play cards at the tables. Others tug on slot machines or try their luck at the roulette wheel. Many scramble to a *sports book*.

A sports book is a place where a bet can be made on a sporting event. Casinos did not always

Gambling clubs were popular in Las Vegas in the 1930s.

have sports books. Casino owners were not sure if they could make a profit against sports bettors. For years, sports books were nothing more than one-room shacks squeezed in along the Strip between liquor stores and souvenir shops. In 1975, the Union Plaza Hotel in downtown Las Vegas opened the first casino sports book. The Stardust Hotel followed a year later. Money flowed through these casino books, profits were made, and other casinos rushed to join in. Most of the small books soon went out of business.

Immediately following World War II, mobster Ben "Bugsy" Siegel built the first plush hotel and casino in Las Vegas and called it the Flamingo. (It has been renamed the Flamingo Hilton.) The Flamingo Hilton operates a typical sports book. It is a lavish, carpeted area at the back of the casino. Along the walls are 53 large televisions that receive signals captured by 14 satellite dishes on the casino roof. Standing behind a counter is a row of employees, known as ticket writers, who are ready to take bets.

ODDS SMORGASBORD

On a wall behind the ticket writers is an enormous electronic board loaded with lighted numbers and names. This is the *odds board*. It is a menu from which to order. Hundreds of people sit in chairs or stand about staring up at this board, almost mesmerized, then step to the counter with money in hand to place their bets. Then they settle in and watch games on the television screens. A snack bar and cocktail service are nearby to help keep bettors there for hours. One minute, a cheer will go up from those bettors whose team just scored a touchdown or hit a home

Ben "Bugsy" Siegel was one of the founders of Las Vegas's gambling industry. He didn't live long enough to see how popular the town became. He was killed in a dispute with his business partners, who were reputed to be criminals.

```
         NATIONAL LEAGUE - SATURDAY,
BET#  TEAM         PITCHER       LINE    12
EVEN  PHILLIES     QUANTRILL              13
-110  CARDS        K HILL                 01
903   PIRATES      ERICKS       +165    8.
904   EXPOS        C PEREZ      -175
905   MARLINS      HAMMOND      +143    8.
906   REDS         SCHOUREK     -153
907   METS         MLICKI       +170    8.
908   BRAVES       SMOLTZ       -180
909   CUBS         FOSTER       +129    8.
910   ASTROS       KILE         -139
911   GIANTS       M LEITER     +172    7
912   DODGERS      NOMO         -182
913   ROCKIES      RITZ         +133    8
914   PADRES       HAMILTON     -143
         AMERICAN LEAGUE - SATURDAY,
BET#  TEAM         PITCHER       LINE
+144  BLUE JAYS    JU GUZMAN
-154  YANKEES      M PEREZ
917   RED SOX      WAKEFIELD    -130
918   ORIOLES      KLINGENBEC   +120
919   INDIANS      BLACK        -110
920   WHITE SOX    A FERNANDE   EVEN
921   BREWERS      GIVENS       +110
922   TIGERS       MOORE        -120
923   TWINS        ERICKSON     +145
924   ROYALS       GUBICZA      -155
925   A'S          DARLING      +135
926   RANGERS      PAVLIK       -145
927   ANGELS       FINLEY       +135
```

A casino's sports book features an odds board that shows the odds for current sporting events.

run. The next minute, a roar will go up from another group watching a different game. The crowd lingers all day and all night until the last game ends. Bettors who win can collect within minutes after the game is over. Bettors who lose can simply tear up their tickets. Many do.

The odds board looks like a wall of hieroglyphics to the non-bettor. The board shows bettors the teams that are playing, the team that is expected to win, and how much that team is expected to win by. The team that is expected to win, that is the supposedly superior team, is called the *favorite*. The inferior team is called the *underdog*. All things being equal, most people would bet on the favorite and win most of the time. That means the casino would lose most of the time. The casino would soon go out of business and there would be no more betting. Therefore, things are not kept equal. The underdog is given a handicap, or an edge. This edge will usually even the chances of either side winning. This edge is generally called the *point spread*.

Here's how the point spread works. Suppose the New York Jets are playing the Minnesota Vikings at the Metrodome in

Minneapolis. The Vikings have the home field advantage. Let's assume the Vikings have a perfect 4–0 record and the Jets are winless at 0–4. Most bettors would put their money on the Vikings, right? But what if eight points were added to the Jets' final score (not in the actual game, but for betting purposes). Which team would bettors choose then? The decision becomes more difficult.

For those who bet on Minnesota, the Vikings must win by more than eight points. Suppose the final score is Vikings 17, Jets 10. With the point spread of eight points added to the Jets' side, the final betting score becomes Vikings 17, Jets 18. Those who bet on the Jets win. Bettors on the Vikings lose. On the other hand, if the Vikings win by more than eight points, say 20–10, bettors say that the Vikings "covered the spread." If the Vikings win by exactly eight points, neither side wins and all bets are returned.

THE CASINO NEVER LOSES

How much money does a winning bettor receive? The odds are 11-to-10. That is, a person must bet $11 to win $10. The $1 difference is called the *juice* or *vigorish*. That

is how the casino makes its money. For instance, say a total of $33 is bet on the Vikings and $33 is bet on the Jets. The casino holds $66 until the game ends. Say the Vikings cover the spread. The casino returns Vikings bettors their original $33, plus pays them $30 more (remember, a bettor wins $10 for every $11 bet). The casino keeps the Jets bettors' money. So the casino pays out $63 and keeps the other $3.

That seemingly small $3 profit, multiplied by thousands of bets, is what helps build casinos. Sports books try to set a point spread that will attract an equal amount of money bet on both sides. That way the casino doesn't worry which team wins or loses. The casino may not always win, but it never loses because it automatically receives its vigorish as profit. Casino operators prefer to leave the worrying to the bettors.

The point spread is also used for basketball games. Baseball, tennis, boxing, and golf use another equalizer known as the *money line*. The money line works like this. Say the Atlanta Braves are playing the Giants at Candlestick Park in San Francisco. The Giants are in first place in their division while the Braves are last in theirs.

Also, the Giants have the home field advantage. In order to encourage gamblers to bet on the Braves, an edge must be given. A money line might be set at, say Giants −180 and Braves +160. What does this mean? Instead of wagering $11 to win $10, a bettor must wager $18 to win $10 on the Giants. If the Giants win, he gets back his original $18, plus another $10. A bettor can wager $10 on the Braves to win $16. If the Braves win, she gets back her original $10, plus another $16. Again, after all bets are settled, the casino pockets the difference.

SETTING THE ODDS

How are point spreads and money lines determined? That is the job of the *oddsmaker,* who tries to set a spread or line that will attract equal amounts of betting on each team in a game. Remember, the casino doesn't want to worry about who wins and loses. It prefers to make its money on the juice. In the 1950s, the New York Mafia set the line. In the 1960s, it was made by the Chicago mob. In the 1970s, Bob Martin took over in Las Vegas. Martin was the oddsmaker at the now-defunct Churchill Downs Race and Sports

Book in 1967. He was known as "The Man," and he was so good at generating equal money on both sides that all the sports book operators began to use his line. "Martin is the man who made the game famous in Las Vegas," says longtime casino sports book operator Sonny Reizner.[2] While it is legal to bet in Nevada, it is illegal to place a bet to a Nevada casino from outside the state. Martin was arrested in 1983 for accepting an out-of-state telephone wager. He was convicted and sentenced to 13 months in prison. His odds-making career ended.

Michael "Roxy" Roxborough, who runs a service called Las Vegas Sports Consultants from the 12th floor of the Valley Bank Building just off the Strip, took over for Martin. Roxborough and his staff of eight set lines for every major sport—a week in advance for football games, the morning of the games for basketball, baseball, and hockey. Roxborough's line goes out by computer to his casino sports book customers and about 70 major newspapers around the country.

Roxborough's line is posted each morning on electronic odds boards at the Flamingo Hilton and the other Las Vegas casinos.

THE SUPER BOWL OF BETTING

The Super Bowl is the biggest sporting event of the year in the United States in terms of TV viewership, newspaper coverage, advertising sales—and gambling. Some estimate that more than $3 billion is wagered on the Super Bowl each year. An array of betting choices is available.

Bettors can wager on who will win the game, of course. A line is also set for each half of the game, as well as every quarter—that is, wagers can be made on which team will outscore the other in each half and quarter. Bettors can decide whether the game will be high or low scoring and can bet accordingly on the *total,* the combined score for both teams. A total is also set for each half and every quarter. A total also is set for each team, for the game, either half, or any quarter. In other words, a bettor can wager that the 49ers will score more than seven points in the second quarter, or that the Steelers will score fewer than six in the third period, and so on.

There is a wide assortment of proposition bets. A gambler can wager money on which player will score the first touchdown, kick the first field goal, intercept the first pass, or register the first sack, or whether any of those things will even happen. Other proposition bets

The Super Bowl attracts more fans than almost any other single sports event.

include how many yards a quarterback will pass for, how many tackles a linebacker makes, which running back will gain the most yardage, which tight end will catch more passes, which team will score first, last, and most often, and which team will win the opening coin toss. "People who bet on the coin toss are sick," says one bookmaker, "but at 11-to-10 odds, I'll gladly accept their bet."

Source: Interview by author, San Diego, 4 July 1995.

Immediately, dozens of runners copy the numbers in notebooks, then rush to telephones to report the odds to *bookmakers,* or bookies, nationwide.

Who are these bookies who operate illegally? In the 1950s and 1960s they were mostly mobsters. Not any more. "The bookmakers are not organized crime people," says Deputy Chief Frank Biehler of the New York City Police Department. "They're regular people that live next door to you."[3]

BEING A BOOKIE

Andrew Pepper (not his real name) of San Diego is a typical bookmaker. He is a sports fan who grew tired of losing money to a bookie and decided to become one himself. He is 33 years old, lives in a modest two-bedroom apartment, and spends each day answering his telephone and taking bets. He has about 200 customers, many of them friends. In 1995, he earned more than $60,000 in vigorish. What's more, he doesn't pay taxes on his income because he doesn't report it to the government.

Andrew's business has its share of dangers. First, of course, is his fear of getting caught. Remember, what he is doing is against the law. And then there are the customers. Andrew doesn't know some of them. For that reason, he sometimes has trouble collecting the money they owe him. Also, Andrew has to be sure he takes enough bets on opposing teams so that he will be able to pay off the winning bettors.

The basics of illegal bookmaking are simple. A bettor gets in touch with a bookie and gives the bookie his or her name, address, and phone number. Once the bookie gives the bettor an account number, the bettor is ready for action. The bettor can phone in a bet any time by giving the account number, then stating the team being bet on and the amount of the bet. A typical conversation might go like this.

> *Bettor: "Hello, this is number three-fifty-eight."*
> *Bookie: "Yes, three-fifty-eight. What can I do for you today?"*
> *Bettor: "What's the line on the Orlando Magic–New York Knicks basketball game?"*
> *Bookie: "Orlando is giving six points."*
> *Bettor: "OK. Give me New York plus six points for $50."*

Bookie: "Number three-fifty-eight. New York plus six for $50. You're in action. Anything else?"

Bettor: "That's all for now. Thank you."

If New York loses by less than six points or wins the game outright, the bettor wins $50. If the bettor loses, he or she owes the bookie $55 (remember the 11-to-10 juice). But money does not exchange hands after every bet as it does in casino sports books. The traffic and mail to the bookie's residence might look suspicious. Instead, a *carryover* is established and the bookie keeps an account. A carryover is a set amount of money, say $200, that serves as a limit. At the end of each week, the bookie checks the accounts of his or her bettors. Those who are owed $200 or more are paid. Those who owe $200 or more must pay. Accounts of less than $200 are "carried over" to the next week. Money is not exchanged unless it is over the limit.

Most sports bettors understand their commitment to a debt. They pay. Occasionally, though, a bettor may not pay a debt. Andrew, the bookie in San Diego, says he loses several thousand dollars each year from bettors who refuse to pay him. And there is not much he can do about it. He can't tell the police. "One guy owed me $3,500," Andrew remembers, "and I tried for weeks to find him and make him pay. Then I found out he was sent to jail for two years. So I kissed that money goodbye."[4]

SCHOOL SCANDALS

In 1995, *Sports Illustrated* conducted a survey of college campuses across the country and found illegal bookmaking to be widespread. Among the students interviewed were a 24-year-old senior at the University of Georgia who handled about $75,000 in basketball bets a month, a 23-year-old senior at the University of Florida who operated for four years out of his campus apartment and earned $42,000 one year, and a 24-year-old marketing major at Clemson University who ran a $100,000-a-month betting operation.

Then there was the 21-year-old sophomore at Texas Tech who was connected with five different off-campus bookies in Lubbock, Texas, and said that he knew of at least 200 other students who made bets as well.

WHY MORE BOYS THAN GIRLS BET ON SPORTS

A survey of Minnesota teenagers showed that nearly 90 percent of those surveyed had gambled at least once. Of those, 6.3 percent had become compulsive gamblers. Dr. Durand F. Jacobs, a psychologist who conducted the study, says, "With 1 in every 10 kids already experiencing serious gambling-related problems, that means two to three kids per class!"

No definitive study has been done on how many boys bet on sporting events compared to girls, but it is clear that sports betting is favored more by boys. Jacobs says, "Boys follow their male models—their father, an older brother, an older peer—who might bet on sports. Boys and sports are synonymous."

Valerie Lorenz, director of the National Center for Pathological Gambling in Baltimore, Maryland, says boys have been encouraged more than girls to be competitive at an early age. "Boys pitch pennies or pitch baseball cards when they are young and that is when their gambling starts," says Lorenz. "They play cards in school and then they graduate to sports betting. Girls generally aren't so competitive. When they do gamble, it's more on a social basis like at church bingo."

Lorenz says girls are inclined to bet on sports once they're introduced

The game of pogs is popular with young boys and girls. Players "bet" their pog chips on what chips will land face up.

to such activity. "A compulsive gambler who just checked into our center got introduced to sports betting at age 29," Lorenz says. "She began betting heavily through a bookie, incurred debts, stole from her employer, couldn't pay them back, lost her job, had criminal charges filed against her, and checked into our center. But the point is, she didn't know about sports betting until the age of 29. Once she found out, she was hooked."

Henry Lesieur, an Illinois sociologist and gambling researcher, says, "Boys are more socialized and active in sports." As girls become more active in competitive sports, they are more likely to become involved in sports betting.

"Social conditions are changing and more and more women are watching sports and gambling in general," says Jacobs. "For instance, it's OK now for a woman to go to a racetrack or a dog track alone. Women will take their place in sports betting over time. You can safely say the girls are catching up and closing the gap."

Sources: Interviews by author, 22 May 1996.

The police department is not surprised at such heavy interest in sports betting. Sergeant Tom McDonald of the Texas Department of Public Safety can name 58 illegal bookies in Lubbock County alone. "Nearly every bookmaker in this town," says McDonald, "got his start as a student at Texas Tech."[5]

Some bookies start even earlier. On March 1, 1995, law enforcement authorities busted a sports gambling operation at Nutley High School in Nutley, New Jersey. Student bookies were accepting bets as high as $1,000 per game and using threats of violence and kidnapping to force losing bettors to pay.

"You'd be shocked at how easy it is for kids to get involved in gambling and how many of them do," says Tom Decker, a retired FBI agent who investigated sports gambling. "You and I could go into a bar in Athens, Georgia, right now, and within minutes we'd have the name of a bookie. Within minutes."[6]

Some bettors consult "experts" before deciding how to place their bets. Television analysts explain on pregame shows who they think will win and why. Reporters write features offering myriad statistics.

Many newspapers print the odds on horse races and other sports events.

A sportswriter for *The San Diego Union-Tribune*, whose pro football predictions appeared weekly in Wednesday editions, remembers a time when the predictions were held until Thursday.

"We had people calling in Wednesday morning, demanding to know where the predictions were, saying they had to make their bets right away," says the sportswriter. "When they were told they would have to wait another day, some of them threatened to cancel their subscription to the newspaper. I just did those predictions off the top of my head and these people were staking their money on them."[7]

Sports-betting advice is available outside the mainstream media as well. More than 700 services nationwide offer "expert" opinions on sporting events. A few provide information by mail. Most give their selections by telephone. These services are scams, but bettors on a losing streak often get desperate and try anything. They pay $3.99 a minute to call a 900 number and receive the "Lock of the Week" or a "Guaranteed Winner." The people providing such services often know something about marketing but very little about sports handicapping.

Some gamblers don't bother to check the experts' picks. "The average guy usually bets on the favorite," says Lem Banker, a professional gambler. "Especially when he's stuck and can't make up his mind but wants to get a bet down anyway."[8]

A BET ON ANYTHING

Since there is money to be made off the betting public, bookies offer odds on virtually everything. A *totals,* or *over-under,* is a bet that the combined scores of both teams will be over or under a number established by the odds-maker. Bettors can wager at 11-to-

10 odds that the final score will be over or under the total.

A three-game *parlay* is a wager in which all three teams a bettor picks must win or the bet is lost. The payoff is higher, but the chance of winning is less.

Finally, most bookies offer *propositions,* or *prop bets,* on sporting events. A prop bet is a bet on something other than the final outcome of the event. Four-to-one odds might be given that Jerry Rice will score the first touchdown in a 49ers–Chargers game, with Natrone Means at 5-to-1, or J.J. Stokes at 8-to-1. If Stokes scores the first touchdown, a bettor who bet $1 on him would win $9—the $1 bet plus $8.

On big sporting events like the Super Bowl, bettors can wager money on such propositions as the number of interceptions or fumbles in a game, or whether a safety will be scored. And choices aren't offered for just football games. For the Indianapolis 500 auto race, for instance, bettors can wager on who will finish last, who will get in the first crash, and the number of cars still running at the end of the race. Some people will bet on almost anything related to a sporting event. Who are these people?

CHAPTER THREE

WINNERS AND LOSERS

■

A man walks into the Stardust sports book carrying a briefcase. He shakes hands with a few people he knows, then looks up at the odds board. After a minute, he steps to the counter, opens his briefcase, removes several bundles of money, and hands them to a ticket writer. "Give me the Cowboys," the man says, "for 55 dimes." A *dime* in sports-betting jargon is $1,000. The man has just bet $55,000 on a football game. The man is a professional gambler. He earns his living betting on sporting events.

Lem Banker is a professional gambler. He never bets less than $1,000 on a game. Sometimes he wagers more than $55,000. "Just on people," he says. "No animals. No tables." Banker doesn't like the odds on horse racing or craps, blackjack or roulette. But 11-to-10 odds on sporting events are fine with him. "Football, basketball, baseball, and a few fights," he says. "That's it—that's my job."[1]

In a crowded sports book, Banker and professionals like him are the ones quietly watching the action amidst the cheering and screaming spectators. When the game ends, the professionals hardly twitch. It's difficult even to tell on which side they bet. Very few gamblers make a living at sports betting—for a good reason. "Upward of 90 percent of sports bettors are losers," says Mort Olshan, publisher of *The Gold Sheet,* a sports newsletter. This doesn't mean that 90 percent of bets lose, but that most bettors don't manage their money. When they win, they bet everything on a second or third game. They bet until they lose and, eventually, they always lose.

The difference between winning or losing, collecting or paying, is razor thin. It all comes down to making the correct pick. "People watch ESPN and read a few newspapers and think they're informed to bet," says Wayne Allyn Root, another professional gambler. "I work 12 hours a day during football season, trying to get information, and I win between 57 and 62 percent of the time. How does somebody think he can win by watching *SportsCenter?* He's going to get slaughtered."[2]

What does it take to be a professional sports gambler? Nerves, patience, and skill. A gambler has to be right 52.38 percent of the time to break even. A gambler has to be right 55 percent or higher to

make a living. Says Banker: "You have a better chance of becoming a rock star than becoming a professional gambler."[3]

BETTING ON LUCK

Nearly all bettors, therefore, are amateurs. And, nearly all bettors believe that they know enough about sports to bet and win. They believe they are experts. An old saying tells it all: "Sports betting is a combination of luck and skill. My losses are due to bad luck and my wins are due to skill." As oddsmaker Michael Roxborough puts it, "The wonderful thing about sports betting is that if you win, you know you're an expert. But if you lose, it's because everybody saw somebody fumble on TV."[4]

For most people who gamble, betting is recreation. These are called *social* gamblers. Social gamblers don't bet more than they can afford to lose, and when they've lost "enough," they stop gambling. Social gamblers may bet on their favorite team to show their support. Or a social gambler may join in an office pool for a major sporting event, such as the Super Bowl or the World Series. Roxborough says people often bet with their hearts, not their heads.

"The general public bet their favorite teams regardless of point spreads or published statistics," says Roxborough. "When the Rams play the Colts, Colts fans will bet on the Colts and Rams fans on the Rams, and rational judgment has little to do with it."[5]

Social gamblers have different methods of making picks, like betting only on home underdogs, or teams "due" for a win, or their favorite team. And they certainly bet different amounts of money. Some amateurs bet the minimum of $11 on a game. Some bet more. Some bet a great deal more.

In *SuperBookie*, Art Manteris, the sports book manager at the Flamingo Hilton, tells the story of the "Music Man." James Toback, a Hollywood director, first appeared on the scene in Las Vegas in 1981, when he showed up at the Barbary Coast sports book. "He bopped into the Barbary wearing a headset, listening to music from a Walkman hooked to his belt, carrying a knapsack full of money," remembers book manager Jimmy Vaccaro.[6] Toback made bets at the counter for huge amounts of money: $40,000 on the Pirates; $50,000 on the Dodgers; $80,000 on the Red Sox; $200,000 on the Twins. Then he put on his headset

Michael Roxborough sets odds on a variety of sporting events for the Las Vegas casinos' sports books.

and bopped out the door. That's when Vaccaro gave him the nickname "Music Man."

For the next month, Music Man bopped all over town placing big bets on sporting events. He bet almost $1 million every day. Then the midseason baseball strike hit. Music Man went to the Barbary Coast cashier to collect his winnings from the night before—about $1.5 million. He filled his knapsack and a suitcase full of money, then stuffed wads of $100 bills inside his pants, shirt, socks, and underwear. Bulging with money, he flew back to his home in Los Angeles. The Barbary Coast sent a security guard with him. When the baseball strike ended two months later, Music Man was back. He resumed his betting, and wagered on NFL exhibition games as well. Then, all at once, his gambling spree ended. Nobody knows what happened, but the Music Man was later spotted making small bets.[7]

ADDICTED TO GAMBLING

Was the Music Man a lucky social gambler? Or was he a *compulsive* gambler? There is a difference between social gambling and compulsive gambling. Social gambling is placing an occasional bet, such as with colleagues in an office pool or friends on a golf course. Compulsive gambling is betting steadily, with no real goal except to continue betting. Most compulsive sports bettors first become captivated by the activity when they "win big." They begin to believe that they know more than the oddsmakers. An old sports betting joke goes like this.

A gambler was hopelessly hooked on football betting. Nothing else interested him. Unfortunately, he lost almost every bet he made. Finally, even his bookie felt sorry for him. "You lose all your bets," said the bookie. "Why don't you bet on hockey instead of football?"

"Hockey?" said the gambler in dismay. "But I don't know anything about hockey!"

Compulsive gambling is also called pathological gambling because the American Psychiatric Association classifies it as a psychological disorder. A compulsive gambler is not satisfied with winning. The gambler wants to bet. If the gambler loses, he or she bets more to try to recoup the losses.

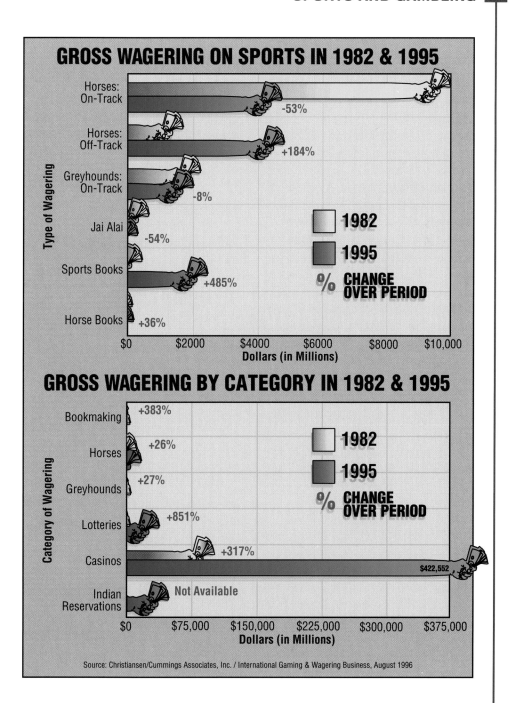

GROSS WAGERING ON SPORTS IN 1982 & 1995

Type of Wagering

- Horses: On-Track — -53%
- Horses: Off-Track — +184%
- Greyhounds: On-Track — -8%
- Jai Alai — -54%
- Sports Books — +485%
- Horse Books — +36%

■ 1982
■ 1995
% CHANGE OVER PERIOD

Dollars (in Millions): $0 $2000 $4000 $6000 $8000 $10,000

GROSS WAGERING BY CATEGORY IN 1982 & 1995

Category of Wagering

- Bookmaking — +383%
- Horses — +26%
- Greyhounds — +27%
- Lotteries — +851%
- Casinos — +317% — $422,552
- Indian Reservations — Not Available

■ 1982
■ 1995
% CHANGE OVER PERIOD

Dollars (in Millions): $0 $75,000 $150,000 $225,000 $300,000 $375,000

Source: Christiansen/Cummings Associates, Inc. / International Gaming & Wagering Business, August 1996

ARE YOU ADDICTED TO GAMBLING?

Compulsive gamblers can't stop gambling. They jeopardize their health, relationships, and futures by continuing to gamble. Often, compulsive gamblers borrow, and even steal, money from friends, relatives, and other people. Even when a compulsive gambler wants to quit, he or she often can't.

Gamblers Anonymous is an organization that helps addicted gamblers. GA is based on Alcoholics Anonymous, in which groups of people meet to discuss their addiction and share advice.

Gamblers Anonymous held its first meeting on September 13, 1957, in Los Angeles, California. Since then, GA has grown steadily throughout the United States and the world. There are nearly 800 chapters in the United States and another 400 in Korea, India, Canada, Australia, and other countries.

Gamblers Anonymous is open to anyone, including teenagers. There is no cost to join. There are also support groups for friends and relatives of compulsive gamblers. Gam-Anon is a group for spouses and friends of gamblers and Gam-Ateen is for the adolescent children of gamblers.

GA asks 10 questions of teenagers to determine the severity of their gambling problem. Most compulsive gamblers will answer yes to at least three of these questions.

1. Have you ever stayed away from school or work to gamble?
2. Is gambling making your home life unhappy?
3. Is gambling affecting your reputation?
4. Do you ever gamble until your last dollar is gone, even your bus fare home or the cost of a burger or a beverage?
5. Have you ever lied, stolen, or borrowed just to get money to gamble?
6. Are you reluctant to spend "gambling money" on normal things?
7. After losing, do you feel you must return as soon as possible to win back your losses?
8. Is gambling more important than school or work?
9. Does gambling cause you to have difficulty sleeping?
10. Have you ever thought of suicide as a way to solve your problems?

Source: Gamblers Anonymous: *Young Gamblers in Recovery,* a publication of Gamblers Anonymous, undated, pp. 1-2.

Gamblers call this *chasing*. A compulsive gambler bets for the rush, not for the money. Compulsive gamblers do not stop gambling even when they run out of money. They find a way to get more money.

Richard J. Rosenthal is a professor of psychiatry at the University of California, Los Angeles, and the president of the California Council on Compulsive Gambling. He says compulsive gambling is "a progressive disorder characterized by a continuous or periodic loss of control over gambling; a preoccupation with gambling and with obtaining money with which to gamble; irrational thinking; and a continuation of the behavior despite adverse consequences." Compulsive gamblers "say they are seeking 'action,' an aroused, euphoric state comparable to the 'high' derived from cocaine and other drugs." Rosenthal says.[8]

Alida Glen, a doctor who counsels compulsive gamblers, says that the gamblers enjoy the high that betting gives them. When they first stop gambling, they want to replace the gambling high with another type of pleasurable experience. Glen says it is difficult to convince them that there isn't a magic solution.[9]

Gil Matro (not his real name) of San Diego is a compulsive gambler. He began gambling at age 10 by flipping baseball cards against garage doors and betting on the way they'd land. He made his first sports bet at age 14 and says he was addicted shortly thereafter. "I lied to my mother, stole money from my grandparents, and practically stopped going to school. All I cared about was betting on sports," Matro says. "I never knew I had a problem until 10 years later when I lost my job and my wife left me. That's when I went to Gamblers Anonymous."[10]

GAMBLERS ANONYMOUS

Gamblers Anonymous is a program, like Alcoholics Anonymous, in which compulsive gamblers enroll to help themselves curb their desire to place bets. Members are buoyed by the strength of others facing the same addiction. "Best phone call I ever made," says Matro. "I never got my wife back, but I got back my sanity. I probably would've been dead today if it weren't for GA."[11]

Why do sports bettors become so desperate? "It [gambling] is every bit as addictive as drugs and alcohol," says Dr. Joe Zieleniewski,

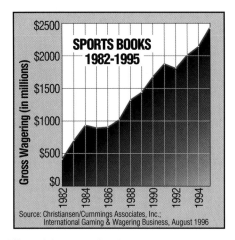

SPORTS BOOKS
1982-1995

Source: Christiansen/Cummings Associates, Inc.;
International Gaming & Wagering Business, August 1996

Nevada's sports books show a dramatic rise in bets placed.

a University of Cincinnati professor and sports psychologist. "For some, betting that first $5 can be like smoking a first joint of marijuana—it can lead to more."[12]

Sports betting is particularly addictive. According to some experts, gamblers are most likely to become addicted to casino games and betting on sports.[13] Sports gambling, card playing, and lotteries are the most popular forms of betting with teenagers.[14]

Compulsive gamblers are often described as intelligent, hardworking, and motivated. They love to meet challenges and take risks, and they crave excitement. Some researchers believe that the younger a person is when he or she starts to bet, the more likely that person is to become a compulsive gambler.[15]

William Jahoda was once a bookmaker for the Chicago Mafia. He says college students are especially vulnerable to sports gambling. "You see gambling on every campus. It is an epidemic," Jahoda says. "These kids are naive. They think that they can do no wrong. They think they're brilliant and they know what they're doing. When you're young, you're invincible."[16] Arnie Wexler, a consultant on sports betting, agrees. "College kids are smart, and I've never met a dumb compulsive gambler. They think they can pick winners, and in the beginning they do. There's always an initial period of success."[17]

The volatile mix of a highly addictive pastime and youthful confidence worries some people. "I see adolescent gambling as being comparable to radon gas," says Harvard psychiatrist Howard J. Shaffer. "It is invisible, odorless and potentially deadly. Gambling is a very reliable and very intense experience that alters the chemistry of the brain."[18]

But other people ask if underage gambling isn't safer than teenage drinking or drug taking.

HITTING ROCK BOTTOM . . . AGAIN

Norm Pecoraro (not his real name) started gambling in high school in Fremont, California, where he blew the $3,000 college savings fund his grandmother had set up for him. In college, he stole money from his brother's catering business to bet on sporting events. In graduate school, he lost $10,000 in student loans through betting and twice robbed a liquor store to help pay off a gambling debt.

Said Norm: "I would borrow money from everyone I knew, make up some crazy story about a family illness or something, just so I could get another bet down. Getting action on a game was a high. Not winning the bet, just making the bet. I never paid anyone back."

By 1991, he had run up debts of $80,000. He joined Gamblers Anonymous. Norm would meet with other compulsive gamblers every Tuesday night at a place called The Gathering Place in Pacific Beach. Family and friends thought Norm was cured, but really he had simply run out of money.

A year later, he raided his wife's $40,000 trust fund and blew the money on horse races and basketball bets. His wife and two-year-old son left him, and an acquaintance

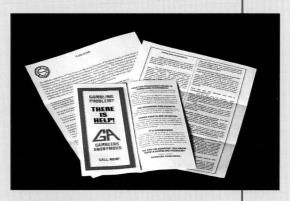

The Gamblers Anonymous organization distributes materials about overcoming an addiction to gambling.

whom he did not repay shattered his knee with a baseball bat. That is why Norm walks with a limp. Finally, he hocked his most precious possession, $2,000 worth of scuba equipment, at a pawnshop and lost the money at the racetrack. That is when he returned to The Gathering Place.

"I hit bottom," says Norm, "and I'm going to be here [Gamblers Anonymous] every week for the next 10 years at least. I need these guys [fellow GA members] more than anyone else in my life. Maybe someday I'll be able to get my wife and son back, too."

Source: Interview by author, Pacific Beach, California, 8 June 1995.

When adults are flocking to casinos, organizing pools, and running fantasy baseball leagues, shouldn't teenagers be able to bet with money they may have earned themselves?

Of course, sometimes problem gamblers get in such a deep hole that they can't "earn" their way out. How bad can life get for young sports gamblers? Take the case of Lyle Ellington, a 21-year-old student at the University of Florida. Lyle began betting in junior high school by going to horse racetracks with older friends. By the time he enrolled at Florida, Lyle was betting hundreds of dollars every weekend on football. He used any money he could get—savings, student loans, financial aid. "The most I ever bet on one game? Twenty-four grand. San Diego Chargers versus Miami Dolphins in 1991," Ellington recalled. When the Chargers scored three late touchdowns, Lyle lost his bet. Then things got worse.

"I took 20 grand from the joint checking account I have with my mom," Ellington said. "I owed, like 35 grand to our neighbor who had bailed me out before. I owed 20 grand to another guy—my mom still doesn't know about that—30 grand to another."[19]

Alex Andrews began betting on sports in high school. He says that by the time he got to college he had become addicted to gambling. "You're unsupervised," he explains. "You can wake up at noon, blow off all your classes, call the bookie at four o'clock, watch all the games while you get drunk, and then do the same thing all over again the next day."[20]

LOVING THE THRILL

For every bettor like Alex Andrews or Gil Matro who recognize their addictions, there are many who believe nothing is wrong. Mike Tyler, a college student at the University of Texas, doesn't think he is headed for trouble. "My first season of gambling was in 10th grade, just small stuff. By the time I was a senior, I won $9,000 in one year," says Tyler. "I'm what you call a successful bettor. I don't mean to glorify gambling, but I love it, and I don't think I'll ever be able to quit. I'll always have a bookie. That won't ever stop. I don't want it to stop. I live by the stroke of luck."[21]

Evel Knievel, a daredevil who once sought thrills by jumping cars and rivers while on a motorcycle, gets his rush through sports betting, especially by betting with his golf playing partners. "I love to feel that knot in my stomach and that lump in my throat," says Knievel. "I live by a credo: The next best thing to gambling and winning is gambling and losing."[22]

There is another saying in the world of sports betting: Win some, lose some, then come back for more. Experts say that anyone who follows this tenet is addicted to gambling. There are plenty of addicts in the United States. And there are some prominent people among them.

Stunt performer Evel Knievel soared over buses during a 1975 show.

Quarterback Art Schlichter seemed headed for a brilliant career when this photo of him was on the cover of *Sports Illustrated* magazine in 1981.

CHAPTER FOUR

IS THE FIX IN?

Art Schlichter was a model quarterback. He was a starter for three years in high school, and his team never lost a game. He started 48 straight games for Ohio State University, set numerous school records, and was an All-America selection. He was the fourth player picked in the 1982 NFL draft. And he was a compulsive gambler.

Schlichter had a promising future in the National Football League. It never happened. By the end of his rookie season with the Baltimore Colts, he was in too deep. He was sick. "Gambling was my outlet, my release," Schlichter said later. "I got high when I placed a bet. Not when I won a bet. When I placed it."[1] Schlichter spent so much time on the phone in the Colts' locker room that his teammates jokingly moved his gear into the phone booth one day. "They thought I was calling girls," Schlichter wrote. "They didn't have the slightest idea I was calling a bookmaker."[2]

Schlichter was watching a basketball game on television with his parents in the rec room of their home in Bloomingburg, Ohio, one night when he hit rock bottom. The Cleveland Cavaliers trailed in

Art Schlichter has been to Gamblers Anonymous meetings, psychiatric hospitals, and prison because of his addiction to gambling.

the game by six points with one second left. Schlichter had a bet on the Cavaliers, getting five and a half points. A Cleveland player was at the foul line, about to shoot two free throws. If he made either shot, Schlichter would win his bet. If he missed both, Schlichter would lose. The bet was for $50,000.

The player missed the first foul shot. Schlichter didn't move a muscle. He didn't speak. His parents didn't even know he was a gambler. He didn't dare tell them. The player missed the second foul shot. Schlichter lost $50,000. "I thought the top was going to blow off my head," he said. "But I didn't flinch. I didn't show any emotion. I just said good night to my mother and father and went to my room, and for the next three hours, I puked. I threw up my guts."[3]

Schlichter kept gambling. Eventually, he completely broke down. He had lost more than one million dollars. He told the NFL about his problem. He told the FBI. He entered a psychiatric hospital. He went to prison for writing bad checks and bank fraud. He joined Gamblers Anonymous. He never played NFL football again.

Art Schlichter was the ideal candidate to be brought down by gambling. Athletes are especially vulnerable to the dangers of wagering. Huge salaries enable them to bet and lose thousands of dollars as if it were Monopoly money. And who has a greater passion for and knowledge of sports than a professional athlete? Still another characteristic that makes athletes susceptible to such a compulsion is their craving for thrills. "Athletes need excitement," says sports psychologist Joe Zieleniewski. "They are sensation-seeking persons. They can become depressed when they aren't thrill-seeking. So gambling, for some of them, is almost a form of therapy."[4]

NFL commissioner Paul Tagliabue opposes legalizing sports gambling.

One study of gamblers revealed that most sports gamblers are middle-class men. They're interested in activities, go to events, play sports, and spend time on recreation.[5] Other studies have shown that compulsive gamblers tend to seek out risks, be competitive, and love excitement. All these characteristics describe many athletes, not all of whom gamble.

However, most people who oppose sports gambling don't do so out of concern for the bettors. Many oppose sports gambling because they believe it would corrupt sports. NFL commissioner

Paul Tagliabue told members of a House Judiciary subcommittee that "Sports gambling inevitably fosters a climate of suspicion about controversial plays and intensifies cynicism with respect to player performances, coaching decisions, officiating calls, and game results."[6]

THE FIX IS IN

Professional athletes have been involved in gambling for generations. In one of the most famous gambling scandals in history, eight members of the Chicago White Sox were accused of fixing the

Joe Jackson, above, was a hero to many baseball fans until he and seven teammates were suspected of deliberately losing a game. They were never convicted of a crime, but baseball commissioner Kenesaw Mountain Landis, next page, banned them from baseball.

1919 World Series. Some players admitted to a grand jury that they purposely lost the Series to the Cincinnati Reds, five games to three. Others forever claimed their innocence. According to Sox first baseman Chick Gandil, he and pitcher Eddie Circotte were told by Arnold Rothstein, a gambler, that if they could get six others to help fix the Series, they would be paid $10,000 apiece. Rothstein figured it would take at least eight players to throw a baseball series. A telegram between gamblers confirmed that the fix was on: "ARNOLD R. HAS GONE THRU WITH EVERYTHING. GOT EIGHT IN."[7]

The odds on the Reds immediately dropped from 3-to-1 to even money, showing that enormous amounts of money were suddenly being wagered on Cincinnati. Sox pitcher Circotte hit the first Reds batter with a pitch, a signal to the others that the fix was on. White Sox manager Kid Gleason and owner Charles Comiskey figured something was up when their players committed numerous errors throughout the Series. But nothing happened until almost a year later when a gambler exposed the fix.

When Shoeless Joe Jackson, an

All-Star hitter and hero to millions, left the grand jury courtroom after testifying, a crowd of boys gathered round their idol. One asked: "It isn't true, is it, Joe?" Shoeless Joe replied: "Yes, boys, I'm afraid it is."[8] Jackson later maintained his innocence, and the case against the eight players eventually was dismissed for lack of evidence. But Kenesaw Mountain Landis, baseball's first commissioner, banned the eight Black Sox—as they became known— from baseball for life.

Historians say that game fixing was a common occurrence in the early part of the twentieth century and that the Black Sox just happened to get caught. A long, inexplicable losing streak by the first-place Louisville Grays in the 1877 season led to the headline "!!!—???—!!!" in the local paper. When the fix became known, baseball's image and popularity suffered until the early 1900s.[9] Just one week before the 1919 World Series, legendary hitter Ty Cobb is believed to have fixed a game.

Pitcher Dutch Leonard, Cobb's Detroit Tiger teammate, said that he and Cobb, along with Tris Speaker and Smokey Joe Wood of the Indians, had met beneath the stands in Detroit and made a deal

Baseball Hall of Famer Ty Cobb was also accused of fixing games.

in which the Indians would deliberately lose to the Tigers the next day. Cobb planned to bet $2,000 on the game, Leonard $1,500, and Speaker and Wood $1,000 each.

Cleveland lost, 9–5, but Cobb didn't make his bet in time, and the others bet less than they planned. When the story was revealed by Leonard, the other three denied it. But Leonard produced two incriminating letters written to him. Wood had written, "If we ever have another chance like this we will know enough to try to get [our bets] down early." Cobb had written, "Wood and myself are considerably disappointed in our business proposition."[10]

Perhaps because of professional baseball's history, team owners have maintained a hard line against gambling. Baseball rules state that anyone employed in the sport who is found guilty of betting on a baseball game is subject to suspension for one year. If the wager involves the player or manager's own team, he faces a permanent ban from the game. The only player in recent times to have been banned from baseball for life was Pete Rose.

Playing infield and outfield for nearly two decades with the Cincinnati Reds, Rose had 4,256 hits—more than any player in major league history. For five years, beginning in 1984, he was the Reds manager. For much of that time, Rose was found to have bet on baseball, including Reds games. His fingerprints were found on a bookmaker's baseball betting slips. Still, Rose denied the allegations, saying, "I'd be willing to bet you, if I was a betting man, that I have never bet on baseball."[11] Rose admitted having bet on football and basketball games

The Cincinnati Reds' Pete Rose is remembered for getting more hits than any other player and for being barred from baseball because he bet on games.

and horse races since 1975, but he denied ever having bet on baseball games. But the evidence was too overwhelming—40 witnesses testified against him—to ignore. One bookmaker said Rose told him, "They can't get me. What have they got? What are they going to prove? How are they going to prove it?" Another bookie said Rose owed him $400,000 and called the hitting star "just a sick gambler."[12] On August 24, 1989, Rose was officially banned from the game he loved.

A public outcry rang out in the summer of 1989 as baseball commissioner Bart Giamatti was about to suspend Rose. A *Time* magazine/CNN network poll showed that only 30 percent of those polled thought Rose should be suspended from baseball for life, while the remaining 70 percent said he should be suspended for just one year or not at all.

Support for Rose was especially strong in Cincinnati, where he was a hero. (Riverfront Stadium, where the Reds play, stands on Pete Rose Way.) Giamatti suspended Rose for life, as baseball rules dictate. But America's tolerance for gambling—as shown by a typical telephone caller to a radio talk show who said, "It's not

Despite pressure to allow Pete Rose to stay involved with baseball, former commissioner Bart Giamatti, above, banned him from the game in 1989.

like he's a criminal or anything"— was clearly revealed.[13]

Despite their adamant stance against players betting on baseball, many baseball team administrators look the other way when players gamble or bet on other sports. In March 1991, Philadelphia Phillies outfielder Lenny Dykstra testified in a Mississippi trial against a man who was charged with running an illegal high-stakes poker operation. Dykstra admitted under oath that he had written checks totaling $78,000 to cover his poker and golf losses. It was a surprise to the public but not to Dykstra's teammates, who knew the gritty centerfielder loved to gamble. Dykstra had not technically violated any of baseball's rules and was placed on probation.[14]

Philadelphia Phillies president Bill Giles says, "I am not concerned by card playing, playing golf for money, basketball pools, betting at the track or shooting dice at a casino."[15] Most players agree that such an attitude by their bosses is necessary. That's because many baseball players are involved in some form of gambling. "If they decided they wanted to go after everyone who plays cards and makes a little wager on it, then nobody would be able to field a team," former Phillies infielder Wally Backman says.[16]

GETTING IN THE POOL

A favorite pastime is competing in pools involving other sports teams. Basketball teammates bet against one another on the NFL playoffs; football players bet with each other on the baseball playoffs and World Series; baseball players participate in pools in-

volving the NCAA basketball tournament and the Indianapolis 500. For instance, the Atlanta Braves operate an NCAA tournament pool each year in which the entry fee is $100, the pot is $6,400, and the winner's check is $5,000. Everybody on the team participates. Federal Bureau of Investigation representatives toured baseball spring training camps in March 1988 to lecture players about the dangers of gamblers and gambling. The representatives arrived one day in Vero Beach, Florida, to address the Los Angeles Dodgers. The FBI agents were told to wait. Their lecture had to be delayed 15 minutes so the L.A. players could finish making their bets in the team's NCAA basketball tournament pool.

How can athletes get away with such gambling? Some types of betting, such as pools and card playing, are legal. By law, a bet is illegal only if there is a fee collected when it's placed. It is not illegal if, say, 20 people put money in a pot and then divide it. This is simply an exchange of money with no fee involved. Even FBI supervisor Tom French admits, "It's possible that a baseball player who runs a clubhouse pool, the guy who collects the money, could be afoul of the law. A pool could be construed as a lottery and certain taxes are involved. But, hey, nobody is going to arrest him."[17] Likewise, it is not illegal if two people make a bet on the golf course. And it's a good thing for NBA superstar Michael Jordan that this is so. Jordan admits having lost hundreds of thousands of dollars in bets on the golf course.

Jordan was leading the Chicago Bulls to their third consecutive NBA championship when a man named Richard Esquinas declared that the three-time MVP had lost golfing bets to him totaling more than $1 million. Although Jordan didn't deny that he had bet on golf games, he said he did not know how much he had lost but that it was much less than Esquinas claimed.

Richard Esquinas accused his former friend, Michael Jordan, of gambling on sports events.

Esquinas, who had been a friend of Jordan's, later claimed that he was at Jordan's home in Chicago one day when he overheard Jordan tell someone on the telephone, "So you're saying the line is seven points." Esquinas, who was watching a basketball game on television with Jordan, says Jordan then turned his back and whispered into the phone for 30 seconds before hanging up. "I can't tell you a bet was placed,"

Chicago Bulls superstar Michael Jordan denies that he bets on sports events.

Esquinas said. "But there is a distinct impression in my mind that Jordan was discussing a betting line."[18]

Jordan denies ever having placed a bet with a bookie. It has never been proved. Jordan retired after the 1992–93 season amid rumors that he had a gambling problem. After attempting a professional baseball career, he returned to the NBA in 1995.

NBA commissioner David Stern is vigilant for possible gambling violations among basketball players. In January 1990, Stern wasted no time in fining Charles Barkley (then playing for the Philadelphia 76ers) and Mark Jackson (then with the New York Knicks) for making $500 wagers with each other linked to their play.

The bet between them stated that any time one of them made

David Stern, the commissioner of the National Basketball Association, has tried to keep NBA players from gambling.

the winning play in a 76ers–Knicks game, the other would have to pay him $500. When Barkley hit the winning shot of a 113–111 Philadelphia victory, the two players told reporters that Barkley had won $500 from Jackson. (Jackson had won $500 from Barkley in a playoff game the previous season.)

When Stern read about the wager in the next morning's papers, he was swift to administer $5,000 fines to each player. "While I am persuaded that there was nothing more going on here than some verbal jockeying between two friendly rivals," Stern announced, "it is my responsibility to make it plain to Barkley and Jackson and everyone else in the NBA that on the subject of gambling, even the slightest appearance of impropriety is a serious matter."[19]

AMATEUR FIXES

Gambling corruption has not been limited to professional sports. Some college athletes have bet on and fixed games as well. Others have had the opportunity but declined. In 1950, the men's basketball team from City College of New York became the first team to win the National Invitation

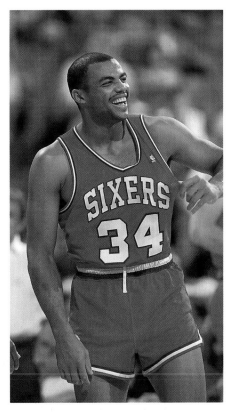

While Charles Barkley was playing for the Philadelphia 76ers, he was fined for gambling about his performance with another NBA player.

FALLING INTO A NIGHTMARE

Chet Forte was an All-America basketball player from Columbia University who became the director of ABC-TV sports. He directed the television show, *Wide World of Sports,* and the network's coverage of the Olympics and heavyweight championship fights.

In 1970, Forte helped create what has become a sports institution—*Monday Night Football.* He transformed football telecasting into a visual spectacle with innovations like sideline cameras, and he was the voice inside the headsets of announcers Frank Gifford, Howard Cosell, and Don Meredith.

Forte became a celebrity. Cosell was his best friend and the best man at his wedding in 1977. Forte earned $900,000 a year at ABC. He considered himself an expert on pro football. And he began betting on games.

For several years, Forte bet his entire salary and lost it. Then he gambled away his savings. The more he bet, the more he lost. He borrowed money from his friends and couldn't pay them back. Still he continued betting on football. He lost his home in New Jersey. He went $4 million in debt. Finally he was arrested for tax evasion.

In 1991, Forte took a job as a local radio sports talk show host. His

Chet Forte orchestrated ABC-TV's Monday Night Football broadcasts before his addiction to gambling led to his arrest for tax evasion.

glamorous life had ended but so had his nightmare. "I'm more happy than I've ever been in my life," he said in 1995. "Purely and simply, it is because I don't gamble. What I went through scared me and my family to death. I'm just trying to be a better person." Chet Forte died a year later.

Source: Chet Forte, "Monday Night Football's Old Loose Cannon Fires Again," *Sport,* February 1995, p. 48.

Tournament and the National Collegiate Athletic Association tournament in the same season. But players from that team were implicated in a *point-shaving* scandal. They had tried to hold down the margin of victory so they wouldn't cover the point spread. In 1985, three men's basketball players at Tulane University were involved in a point-shaving conspiracy.[20]

University of Florida quarterbacks Kyle Morris and Shane Matthews were suspended midway through the 1989 season for betting on college football. But Florida alumni proudly tell the story of Honest Jon MacBeth. One night in August 1960, MacBeth was approached by two gamblers who offered him $5,000 to shave points in a game against rival Florida State. As Florida's main running back, MacBeth could deliberately fumble the ball in key situations of the game. But MacBeth did not accept the bribe. Instead, he turned the gamblers down, then helped bust them by cooperating in a police sting operation that resulted in the gamblers' convictions.[21]

University of Arkansas officials were embarrassed by a campus betting scandal in 1989 when po-lice arrested senior Mike Grace, a brother of Chicago Cubs first baseman Mark Grace, for bookmaking. The list of about 150 alleged clients was found to include the names of six Razorback athletes, including a basketball player and three baseball players. The Arkansas chancellor asked professor Al Witte, Arkansas faculty representative for athletics who was serving as NCAA president at the time, to look into the matter. Witte made an embarrassing discovery. His son, Robert, a 27-year-old Arkansas graduate, and the chancellor's son, Sean Ferritor, a 20-year-old sophomore, were two of Grace's betting clients. Sean Ferritor said his father "was not pleased" with the news.[22]

BETTING ON HIGH SCHOOLS

Even high school sporting events are not free of gamblers. In July 1989, local police and FBI authorities in Florence, Alabama, uncovered evidence that games may have been fixed. Florence police chief Rick Thompson said that coaches and officials had been "manipulating the outcome of high school sporting events to cover the point spread by oddsmakers." Seven homes were raided, including those of two assistant football coaches. Police seized betting sheets and more than $100,000 in cash. Evidence showed that someone had tampered with equipment, such as game clocks and yardage markers. Authorities were disturbed that lines had been established and bets made on high school games. They were even more distressed that games might have been fixed, although that charge could not be proven.[23]

Still, that pales in comparison to what happened in New York City a year earlier. Police discovered that drug dealers were recruiting promising neighborhood players, luring them with cash and $80 sneakers to play in playground tournaments on which the dealers placed big bets. Gregory Vaughn, a high school coach who worked with inner-city youth in his spare time, was asked to referee a neighborhood game. When Vaughn made some calls that angered the gamblers, he was followed off the playground and murdered. The stakes in the game were about $50,000.[24]

Are many games at any level fixed? Probably not. It is not easy persuading high school or college athletes to jeopardize their futures and pro athletes to risk their careers for the sake of some fast money. In fact, at the professional level, outrageous salaries might serve in this case to make sports cleaner. What $1-million-a-year athlete would jeopardize his earnings by fixing a game? Also, as oddsmaker Roxy Roxborough points out, "If there was widespread corruption in sports, there wouldn't be any bookmakers left. If there's no integrity, nobody's going to bet."[25]

The fact remains that athletes bet. Might a player be willing to trade inside information about his team ("the starting pitcher's arm is sore; the quarterback might be benched") for the cancellation of a bookmaking debt, or even for cash?

"Naive people think an athlete who's making millions of dollars wouldn't consider doing something like that for, say, $50,000," says FBI supervisor Tom French. "But if he has a heavy-spending lifestyle, well, that $50,000 or $100,000 is a tax-free thing."[26] As Dave Nightengale writes in *The Sporting News* about baseball: "Could the outcome of a major league baseball game actually be fixed in this day and age? Don't bet on it, but don't bet against it."[27]

WHAT ARE THE ODDS . . .

- Of being struck by lightning in a lifetime? **1 in 600,000.**
- Of winning a lottery with a single ticket? **1 in 5,200,000.**
- Of owning a car? **United States, 66 in 100. Vietnam, 1 in 10,000.**
- Of being a genius (an IQ above 139). **1 in 250.**
- Of a high school student studying more than an hour a day? **9 in 25.**
- Of dropping out of high school before graduating? **1 in 10.**
- Of a high school football player making it to the NFL? **1 in 1,175.**
- Of a high school football player playing quarterback in a Super Bowl? **1 in 100,000.**
- Of a pro golfer sinking a hole in one on a given day? **1 in 3,708.**
- Of being injured in an automobile accident this year? **1 in 75.**
- Of being hit by a baseball at a major league game? **1 in 300,000.**
- Of being killed in an air crash? **1 in 460,000.**
- Of drowning in the bathtub? **1 in 685,000.**
- Of a 13-year-old eating a fast-food hamburger on a given day? **1 in 29.**
- Of a 13-year-old watching television on a given day? **1 in 3.**
- Of being lefthanded? **1 in 10.**
- Of giving birth to twins? **1 in 90.**
  Triplets? **1 in 9,000.**
  Quadruplets? **1 in 900,000.**
  Quintuplets? **1 in 85 million.**
- Of undergoing a heart transplant? **1 in 3,048.**
- Of making money as a regular racetrack bettor? **1 in 100.**
- Of making money, long-term, as a sports gambler? **1 in 5,000.**

Sources: Les Krantz, *What the Odds Are* (New York: HarperCollins, 1992). Bernard Siskin, *What Are the Chances?* (New York: Crown Publishers, Inc., 1989).

CHAPTER FIVE

SHOULD ALL BETTING ON SPORTS BE LEGAL?

So many people enjoy gambling on sports that some people think it should be legal everywhere. After all, these advocates say, other forms of gambling are legal in many states, and sports gambling is legal in some states. If gambling on sports were legal everywhere, the government could regulate and tax those who participate. That way, gambling would be controlled and run cleanly, and all people would benefit from the tax money that was raised.

While most people turn a blind eye to sports betting, there are those who cringe when they hear people like New York Mets executive vice president Frank Cashen say, "Gambling by the players is nothing I'd lose three minutes' sleep over. I am not the players' keeper."[1] They shudder when they pick up the newspaper and see the spreads on pro and college games prominently displayed next to ads touting betting services. Indiana basketball coach Bobby Knight poses an interesting question when he asks: "Why don't the newspapers run hookers' phone numbers? Is betting on basketball, football or baseball less illegal than prostitution?"[2] (Others point out that newspapers do print ads for "singles" and for "escorts.") Those who oppose legalizing gambling on sports point out that social gambling can easily develop into a serious problem. For some, it could become an addiction. Should the government contribute to a potential tragedy?

Thirty-seven countries around the world operate—and tax—popular sports pools. England has had legal sports betting shops since 1960. What should the United States do? Mike Orkin says in his book *Can You Win?*, "If betting on football is legal in Nevada and Oregon, why should it be illegal elsewhere? Billions are bet illegally. Why not give states a cut of the action? Sports betting is a recreational activity enjoyed by people from all backgrounds. You can bet in the stock market on the success (or failure) of a company. Why shouldn't you be able to bet on the success of a football team without risking a jail term?"[3]

Sports Illustrated's William Oscar Johnson writes, "It isn't a question of whether we should legalize sports gambling in the U.S. It is a question of why we have been so stupid as to leave this lucrative and hugely popular segment of sport to the Mob and the office pool for so long. The great American gambling pot should be tapped—now—to help bail out our debt-ridden governments."[4]

When the former president of the North American Association of State and Provincial Lotteries testified before a House subcommittee, he told them that sports lotteries could be an answer to many social problems. "State-sponsored sports-pool lotteries could raise hundreds of millions in new non-tax revenue for the important state-run programs funded by lotteries, including education, economic development, senior citizen programs and state general funds," James E. Hosker said.[5]

TOO MUCH BETTING

The opponents of legalized sports gambling argue that more legal gambling won't raise significant money for social programs. In fact, they say, there may already be a glut of gambling opportunities. As one example, the antigambling forces point out that after the increase of casinos and slot machines, attendance at racetracks went down 3.7 percent in 1991 and nearly 4.1 percent in 1992.[6] They say that gambling,

Some advocates of legalized gambling argue that what stockbrokers and commodities traders do on the stock exchange is a form of gambling. Instead of betting on teams, investors bet on companies.

particularly gambling on sporting events, is very addictive, especially for young gamblers. They fear that legalized gambling would corrupt sports and ruin fans' enjoyment of events.

Professional league administrators are firmly against gambling on their games. NFL commissioner Paul Tagliabue says that legal wagering would distort the image of professional sports so much that the public would view professional athletes as "out to get the fast buck, the quick fix, the desire to get something for nothing." NBA commissioner David Stern warns that legalized sports gambling would "transform the betting line into the bottom line" and that fans would "begin to leave games feeling disappointed or cheated even though their team has won." Former baseball commissioner Fay Vincent says that "the legalization of team sports betting by any state or municipality would increase the chances

FOR A HOT TIP,
CALL 1-900-SCAM

One by-product of the surge in sports betting is the 1-900 telephone line. "Betting experts" tell callers what teams to bet on at a cost of $3.99 a minute or more. Some "top handicappers" charge as much as $50 per phone call for their picks.

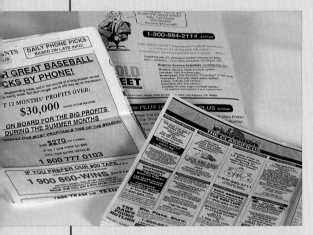

The search for "a sure thing" leads gamblers to look for advice from betting services.

There are more than 700 such services nationwide available to anyone with a telephone. Because they say their information is for "entertainment purposes only," hotline operators are not regulated by any government or independent group.

David James was a "betting expert." For three years, James offered his weekly football picks to anyone who wanted to hear them. A lot of people listened. In 1993, hundreds of gamblers spent over $60,000 to receive James's National Football League selections. Advertising himself in national sports publications as "The Wiz Kid: Bookies hate him! You will love him!," James offered his choices to sports bettors desperate for that special information that would make them winners. The catch was, James knew nothing about football. "This is a country where people read *The National Enquirer* and *The Weekly World News* and believe a woman gave birth to a 100-pound baby," James says. "Why shouldn't they believe me?" Plenty of bettors did.

James accompanied his Wiz Kid ads with a high school photo that made him look like a bright, new handicapper who used unique high-tech methods for calculating winners. "I had my four-year-old son make the picks," James admits. James would place a newspaper in front of his son, and his son would point arbitrarily to different teams. "The team he picked went on the line," James confesses. "I'd just make up some bogus statistic to justify his selection: wind conditions on the field—you know, stuff that was totally un-checkable."

James used phrases such as "Sure Thing!," "Guaranteed Winner!," "Lock of the Decade!," and "Game of the Year!" to convince compulsive gamblers the predictions were solid. The first week, James's son picked one game correctly. The second week he picked all eight correctly. The Wiz Kid's call volume tripled. By the fourth week of the season, James was charging $25 per call. And bettors were paying.

In January 1994, James ended his service. He didn't feel guilty contributing to the addiction of gamblers, and he wasn't concerned about other people losing money, even when he received a death threat. James says he quit because he found himself becoming emotionally attached to his son's picks. He was rooting for the winners to come in, feeling just like a bettor himself. He knew then that it was time to get out.

James says he learned a lot about 1-900-line sports betting services, and especially about gamblers, during his three-year stint. "Such as, the more you charge, the better they think you are," James says. "Such as, nobody ever asks for documentation of the claims made in your advertisements.

"Such as, the clientele for a 900-line that purports to be able to pick winners in a football game is so sick that even if you lose they won't stop calling you. If you win, great! They love you. You're a genius. And if you happen to lose, they figure you can't be wrong twice, so they call you again, get the next game and double their bet. Thursday night ESPN game, they bet $100 and lose. Saturday morning college, $200; afternoon game, $400. Now they're probably stuck close to a grand. Sunday morning maybe they bet three games at $300 apiece, all based on my predictions, then sometimes another $1,000 on the late game. And then, if they're still stuck, the big bailout game. I got more calls for the Monday night game than all the other games combined."

Source: Michael Konik, "1-(900) N-F-L S-C-A-M," *Forbes*, 21 November 1994, pp. 119-121.

that persons gambling on games will attempt to influence the outcome of those games."[7]

SOME SPORTS WANT BETS

In contrast, professional boxing and horse racing have always relied heavily on sports betting to generate enough interest to survive. And those aren't the only sports to recognize the appeal of gambling. At the 1995 Reno Air Games, a meet staged each year in Reno, Nevada, USA Track & Field (USATF) officials persuaded the Eldorado Race and Sports Book in Reno to set odds and take bets on the meet. "We had to introduce new elements to make track more entertaining to the casual fan," said meet director John Mansoor. In other words, the USATF tried to boost the sport's sagging popularity by encouraging gambling. Before the meet, the athletes were required to sign a statement saying they would not place any bets, even on themselves, "to protect the meet's integrity," said Mansoor.[8]

Some opponents of legalized sports gambling are all too aware of the appeal of betting. They worry that legal betting would overshadow the importance of

Boxing is one sport that has always generated many bets.

the game or event itself. Boston Celtics president Arnold "Red" Auerbach told a Congressional subcommittee that legal gambling would hurt sports. "Legalized sports betting creates a new type of fan—the 'point-spread' fan who is more concerned with whether the point spread is covered, not whether his team wins or how the players perform. Games are not entertainment events but only activities from which they hope to profit."[9]

Former National Hockey League (NHL) president John Ziegler took action in September 1989 to head off any problems with gambling. Rotisserie League Baseball and other sports fantasy leagues are contests in which participants select rosters of pro players and compete against one another, using the statistics those players amass in real games. Ziegler sent a memo to NHL team officials declaring that the league's antigambling policy forbids them to take part in any fantasy hockey league played for money.

Was Ziegler's action extreme? Would a hockey general manager get so carried away in a fantasy league that he would make a real-life trade or tell his coach to bench a player just to help his

Fay Vincent, former baseball commissioner, says that allowing some gambling on sports will lead to more illegal gambling.

fantasy team? The NHL commissioner didn't want to find out.

Major League Baseball has taken precautions as well. The caretakers of the game don't wish to see small-time betting develop into big-time problems. As former commissioner Vincent warns: "Just as a little marijuana can go to cocaine to heroin, then so can a little bet go to a big bet to indebtedness. And indebtedness to a big bookie usually means the involvement of the Mob. And they are bad people to know."[10]

To combat possible links to criminals, baseball employs not only FBI representatives to warn players of the dangers, but also FBI special agents, one for each ballpark. Jack Ballentine patrols Candlestick Park in San Francisco, on the lookout for gamblers and bookies.

"The potential for unsavory people hanging around celebrities is high, and with unsavory people, there's always a potential for gambling and drugs," Ballentine says. "I can't save the rich kids [baseball players] from themselves, but I try to make sure they aren't surrounded by sharks."[11] FBI agents prowl the parking lot, the stands, the locker rooms, anywhere the gamblers might try to get to the people who could fix games for them. "If you don't go into the locker room three or four times a week," Ballentine says, "just to see who's hanging around the players, umpires and managers, then you leave open one door that shouldn't be left open."[12]

CRIMINAL ELEMENTS

Those who want evidence of organized crime's ties with sports gambling got it during the winter of 1992. Four mobsters and two bystanders were murdered in Brooklyn, New York, in a series of revenge killings involving the Colombo crime family. Instead of patrolling every street corner in

the city for assassins, the Brooklyn police decided to send a message to the Colombo mob. Two weeks before the Super Bowl, the police shut down the mob's number one business—gambling. In a sting that took several days, police served 60 search warrants, arrested 100 mobsters, and confiscated $1.5 million in cash and equipment. The Colombo bookmakers couldn't take any bets. The criminals took the hint. The killings stopped. Eventually, the gambling operation resumed. The shootings did not.[13]

On the other side of the country, police in northern California raided buildings in Oakland, Alameda, and Brisbane, along with a headquarters in the Dominican Republic. They shut down an enormous sports gambling ring in which customers phoned in bets by dialing an 800 number from anywhere in the United States, and debts were paid by Federal Express overnight delivery or through international banks. The operation was handling an estimated $100 million a month, or $1.2 billion a year, in wagers.[14]

Even the smallest of operations can be shut down. On September 18, 1989, police in Austin, Texas, may have conducted the first fan-

Members of the Colombo family in New York were accused of running an illegal sports gambling operation, in addition to other criminal activities.

tasy league bust. They arrested eight men in a bar for participating in a fantasy football league. The gamblers were charged with a second-degree felony of engaging in organized crime, which is punishable by up to 20 years in prison and a fine of $10,000. (The men did not receive a harsh sentence.) Police said each man paid a $250 entry fee, and the winner stood to make as much as $3,000 at the end of the season. The men claimed the winner would get only a trophy. The police were responding to a call from the wife of

one of the men. The wife complained that her husband had spent part of the rent money on his entry fee. "I've had people say gambling is a victimless crime," said police sergeant Byron Cates, "but if a guy is out there betting and losing money so kids have to go without food or shoes, that's not victimless."[15]

The Austin bust was a rare exception, however, to the way law enforcement authorities treat gambling. In the book *Collision at Home Plate,* author James Reston Jr. writes about the FBI of the

1980s. "The Bureau found that to bust mom-and-pop gambling operations all over the country might help statistics but made no dent whatever in organized crime."[16]

LEGAL VS. ILLEGAL

Some argue that people who are already gambling on sports would not switch from their illegal bookies to legal games because the bookies let them bet on credit and don't take out money for taxes. These opponents argue that legalizing gambling on sports would create additional gamblers, most of whom would be teenagers. Valerie Lorenz of the Compulsive Gambling Center in Baltimore, Maryland, says that sports are "uniquely attractive" to young people. "The knowledge that children would acquire through sports lotteries would quickly lead them to illegal sports gambling, once they also discover the greater odds and thrill of risk such illegal gambling offers."[17]

The government supports some forms of gambling, but has largely curbed gambling on sports. In June 1992, the U.S. Senate voted 88 to 5 to bar states from permitting gambling on professional and amateur sporting events.

Opponents of gambling protest the government's involvement in more gambling operations.

A SUCCESS STORY

Doug is a 20-year-old college student who grew up in the San Francisco Bay Area. As a teenage sports fan, he started making small bets on his favorite teams. Before he knew it, he was a compulsive gambler. Here is his story.

One day, when I was 14, my dad brought home this football pool sheet. My dad was a teacher at a high school across town, and there were about 40 teachers in the pool. It was real simple. You picked the winners of 15 college games and 10 pro games. Whoever picked the most winners won the $40 pot. It cost a dollar to enter. This was my introduction to gambling.

After a few weeks of doing this with my dad, I was hooked. I could hardly wait until Wednesday when he came home with that week's pool sheet. Since we disagreed on some games, he started letting me do my own picks, and we turned in two sheets. One time I won. It was an incredible rush.

The following year, they weren't going to have the pool. My dad said the guy who ran it, I think it was a math teacher, didn't want to run it again. I convinced my dad that I could run it. I could type up the weekly sheets, make copies, track the results, do everything. All my dad had to do was take the sheets to work and pass them around. I talked him into doing it.

Running that pool was so much fun that I started one at my own high school the next year. There must've been a hundred students, and some teachers, too, competing in my weekly pool. I became known as a football expert. Really, I was a bookie. The whole school knew about it. The principal didn't bet because he didn't know football, but the vice principal did.

That same year, I got hooked up with a big-time bookie. I was convinced I knew as much about football as anybody. I loved making picks. But the thrill of betting a dollar a week in a pool had worn off. I wanted to bet more, maybe $20 a game. So I met this guy at school, a senior, who knew a bookmaker. I never knew the bookmaker's name, but I talked with him on the phone a lot. Other guys at school bet through him, too. Most of us just called him Mr. X.

I would call Mr. X on the phone and say, "Hello. This is Doug, number two-four-seven," and then I'd tell him my picks for the week and how much I wanted to bet on each pick. The minimum bet on a game was normally $30, but he knew I was a kid so he usually gave me a break and let me bet as low as $10 on a game. Once in a while, though, he was in a bad mood and wouldn't accept any bet less than $30. In those cases, I bet the $30 because I needed to make the bet.

The funny thing was, I did pretty well at first. I won money, over $400, my first couple of months. He paid me through the guy at school, the senior, who had hooked me up.

When football season ended, I started betting on baseball games. I was betting almost every day now. I would bring the sports section to school and figure out my picks in class. Then at lunchtime, I would drive home with my buddies and call in my bets. Or I would just call them in from the school pay phone. One time, when the pay phone was being used and lunch period was about over, I panicked and used the school office phone. I told the secretary it was an emergency. I turned my back to her and whispered my bets to the bookie. She didn't have a clue what I was doing.

I got so obsessed with betting that I would load up on the local game, either the Oakland A's or San Francisco Giants, and then drive with my friends or take [public tran-

sit] to the game. If it was a day game, starting at 1 o'clock, I would leave school at lunch and not come back. I would bet big on the game, like maybe $100. The trouble was, I would almost always bet on the A's or Giants, because I was a fan, and the bookie knew it so he would fudge the odds against me. For instance, it would say in the paper that the A's were a slight favorite, but he would say they were a heavy favorite and make me bet more to get the same return. I would bet it anyway. I was stupid.

I started losing badly. I worked at a toy store, loading and unloading boxes and stuff, and my paychecks started going to the bookie. Then I began betting more to try to get my money back. I was betting $50 or more on games I knew nothing about. This got me in a deeper hole. Eventually, I wiped out a college savings account of $2,000. My parents never knew, because if they had, they'd have killed me.

I got more and more in debt. I kept betting anyway. Football season started up again and I ran the pool at school, just so I could skim money off the top. I would get 120 people in the pool in a week, and then say there were only 80 who entered so I could keep the other $40 for myself.

I started borrowing money from friends. They knew it was for betting, but I would convince them that I had a sure lock, a guaranteed winner that couldn't lose. I was very good at convincing people.

I also had a good system of borrowing. I would pay back one friend by borrowing more from another. Pretty soon, though, I think I owed half the guys in my class. And they were angry about it.

I started stealing money from my boss. Not much at first, just $20 from the cash register here and there. It was so easy that I started taking more. He must've known what was going on because one day he fired me. I asked him why and he just stared at me. I knew not to argue about it.

I bet basketball and hockey and baseball, and by summertime, I owed the bookie, Mr. X, about $4,000. I didn't have any money, and my friends were all mad at me.

I had to tell my parents the whole story. As you might expect, they hit the roof. They paid Mr. X and then paid off my friends. And then they sentenced me to a life of chores to work the money off.

Believe it or not, I started betting again. I found another bookie, and before long I was about $3,000 in debt. I had to tell my parents again. This time, they weren't as much angry as they were worried.

My parents put me in a rehabilitation program, kind of like Gamblers Anonymous. I had to explain in front of a group of people what happened to me and how I couldn't control sports betting. Each of these people had to tell their stories, too. It's been three years now, and I still go to these meetings about once a month. I've heard the same stories over and over, and they're all sort of like mine, but they help me remember what it used to be like.

When I look back on my teenage addiction, I have to admit that betting was fun at first. It was something that I knew about, something that I was pretty good at, something that my friends at school admired me for. But the fun lasted about two months. After that, it was two years of pure hell. So many nights I went to bed in fear, wondering how I would pay the money I owed. I was scared to death.

I can't ever forget that.

Source: Interview by author, Bloomington, Indiana, 21 April 1995.

Delaware, Montana, Nevada, North Dakota, and Oregon already allowed some form of sports betting at that time, but other states wanting to join the lucrative trade were denied. New Jersey Senator Bill Bradley, a former basketball star with the New York Knicks, said, "This will preserve the opportunity for all young people who want to participate in sports to regard the game as theirs, not the gamblers'."[18]

On the state level, the New Jersey State Assembly blocked a constitutional amendment in late 1993 that would have allowed sports betting in Atlantic City's 12 casinos. The gaming industry sued, but the state supreme court ruled against it.

"We're disappointed that we can't offer our customers sports betting," said New Jersey casino official Tom Bellazzi. "As for the proliferation of riverboat gambling across the country, we believe that this will create opportunities for the industry."[19]

Bellazzi's statement is ominous. While legislators rule against betting in some cases, other times they appear to be triggering the spread of legalized gambling.

After all, the Congress approved riverboat gambling in 1989, just a year after it approved casinos on Native American land and state-run lotteries.

PROS AND CONS

Why stop there? Why not legalize all sports betting everywhere? Huge sums of money certainly would be collected by the government if sports betting were controlled by the state. This money could go to schools, parks, libraries. Bookmakers would not go out of business, but at least some of them would report their income and be taxed on it. Government workers could monitor the athletes, bookmakers, and gamblers to ensure that the games were played fairly and that the gamblers received fair odds. Restrictions could be imposed on how often a person gambled, and how much he or she bet. With the increased revenue from gambling taxes and licensing fees, governments could reduce other taxes.

While some proponents of legalizing gambling recognize that compulsive gambling is a problem for many people, they argue that most gamblers aren't problem gamblers. Why should those for whom gambling is a fun hobby be denied that outlet just because some people abuse the freedom to gamble?

Opponents of gambling point out that compulsive gamblers don't just hurt themselves, they hurt their families, their employers, and those around them. Gambling, they say, is not just a personal issue—it is a community and societal issue. Compulsive gamblers are more likely to commit crimes, have accidents, do poor work, and be sick or injured.

Gambling critics say that gambling revenues won't raise enough money to cover the added social costs of the criminal and physical needs of those affected by the increased gambling. Gambling opponents also argue that more gambling opportunities mean more gamblers and more problem gamblers. These gamblers won't necessarily limit their gambling to legal bets. As illegal gambling increases, the opportunities for criminals to taint the games people love to play and watch increases. Senator Bradley is among the voices that vehemently oppose the further legalization of sports gambling. "Sports should be about personal and team achievements," Bradley insists, "not about winning or losing money."[20]

New Jersey Senator Bill Bradley has been an outspoken opponent of gambling on sports.

NOTES

CHAPTER 1: PLAYING THE GAME

1. Art Manteris, *SuperBookie: Inside Las Vegas Sports Gambling* (Chicago, Ill.: Contemporary Books, 1991), p. 7.

2. Dave Nightengale, "Baseball's Big-Stakes Game," *The Sporting News,* 1 July 1993, p. 10.

3. John Daly and Solange de Santis, "The Winner Takes It All," *Macleans,* 9 April 1990, p. 50.

4. Frank Deford, "Laying It All on the Line," *Newsweek,* 27 January 1992, p. 54.

5. George J. Church, "Why Pick on Pete?" *Time,* 10 July 1989, p. 20.

6. Blaine Harden and Anne Swardson, "You Bet! It's the $482 Billion National Pastime," *The Washington Post,* 3 March 1996, p. A1.

7. Tim Layden, "Bettor Education," *Sports Illustrated,* 3 April 1995, p. 85.

8. Blaine Harden and Anne Swardson, "States View Addiction as Chance They Have to Take," *The Washington Post,* 4 March 1996, p. A8.

9. Shelagh Donoghue, "The States Like the Odds," *Time,* 10 July 1989, p. 19.

10. Layden, "Bettor Education," p. 71.

11. Hank Wesch, "Friday Nights a Smash at Hollywood Park," *The San Diego Union-Tribune,* 26 May, 1995, p. C1.

12. Church, "Why Pick on Pete?" p. 20.

13. Art Levine, "Playing the Adolescent Odds," *U.S. News & World Report,* 18 June 1990, p. 51.

14. Harden and Swardson, "States View Addiction as Chance They Have to Take," p. A8.

15. Ricardo Chavira, "The Rise of Teenage Gambling," *Time,* 25 February 1991, p. 78.

16. Layden, "Bettor Education," p. 85.

17. Layden, "Bettor Education," p. 85.

18. Henry R. Lesieur and Robert L. Custer, "Pathological Gambling: Roots, Phases, and Treatment," *Annals of the American Academy of Political and Social Science,* July 1984, p. 149.

19. J.M. Fenster, "Nation of Gamblers," *American Heritage,* September 1994, p. 36.

20. Church, "Why Pick on Pete?" p. 20.

21. James Reston Jr., *Collision at Home Plate* (New York: HarperCollins, 1991), p. 242.

22. *Headline News,* Cable News Network, 2 June 1995.

23. Robert McGarvey, "Sports Gambling '90s Style," *Sport,* April 1989, p. 57.

24. William M. Bulkeley and James McNair, "Internet Casinos to Bring Gambling into the Home," *The San Diego Union-Tribune,* 30 May 1995, p. CL8.

25. Manteris, *SuperBookie,* p. 71.

26. James Cook, "If Roxborough Says the Spread is 7, It's 7," *Forbes,* 14 September 1992, p. 363.

27. Manteris, *SuperBookie,* p. 224.

28. William Oscar Johnson, "A Sure Bet to Lower Debt," *Sports Illustrated,* 12 September 1991, p. 144.

29. Tim Layden, "Book Smart," *Sports Illustrated,* 10 April 1995, p. 74.

CHAPTER 2: WHERE THE ACTION IS

1. Walter Wagner, *To Gamble, or Not to Gamble* (New York: The World Publishing Company, 1972), p. 115.

2. Art Manteris, *SuperBookie: Inside Las Vegas Sports Gambling* (Chicago, Ill.: Contemporary Books, 1991), p. 41.

3. James Cook, "If Roxborough Says the Spread is 7, It's 7," *Forbes,* 14 September 1992, p. 354.

4. Andrew Pepper (pseudonym), interview by author, San Diego, California, 4 July 1995.

5. Tim Layden, "Bettor Education," *Sports Illustrated,* 3 April 1995, p. 74.

6. Layden, "Bettor Education," p. 71.

7. Author, San Diego, California.

8. Robert McGarvey, "Sports Gambling '90s Style," *Sport,* April 1989, p. 59.

CHAPTER 3: WINNERS AND LOSERS

1. Robert McGarvey, "Sports Gambling '90s Style," *Sport,* April 1989, p. 57.

2. Tim Layden, "Bettor Education," *Sports Illustrated,* 3 April 1995, p. 80.

3. McGarvey, "Sports Gambling '90s Style," p. 58.

4. Frank Deford, "Laying It All on the Line," *Newsweek,* 27 January 1992, p. 54.

5. James Cook, "If Roxborough Says the Spread is 7, It's 7," *Forbes,* 14 September 1992, p. 358.

6. Art Manteris, *SuperBookie: Inside Las Vegas Sports Gambling* (Chicago, Ill.: Contemporary Books, 1991), p. 102.

7. Manteris, *SuperBookie,* pp. 101-108.

8. Richard J. Rosenthal, "Pathological Gambling," *Psychiatric Annals,* February 1992, pp. 72-73.

9. Stuart Winston and Harriet Harris, *Nation of Gamblers: America's Billion-Dollar-A-Day Habit* (Englewood Cliffs, N.J.: Prentice-Hall, 1984), p. 117.

10. Gil Matro (pseudonym), interview by author, Clairemont, California, 9 March 1995.

11. Matro, interview by author, 1995.

12. Dave Nightengale, "Baseball's Big-Stakes Game," *The Sporting News,* 1 July 1993, p. 10.

13. Chris Welles, "America's Gambling Fever," *Business Week,* 24 April 1989, p. 120.

14. Art Levine, "Playing the Adolescent Odds," *U.S. News & World Report,* 18 June 1990, p. 51.

15. Deborah Crisfield, *The Facts about Gambling* (New York: Crestwood House, 1991), p. 33.

16. Layden, "Bettor Education," p. 76.

17. Layden, "Bettor Education," p. 76.

18. Blaine Harden and Anne Swardson, "States View Addiction as Chance They Have to Take," *The Washington Post,* 4 March 1996, p. A8.

19. Layden, "Bettor Education," p. 76.

20. Layden, "Bettor Education," p. 76.

21. Layden, "Bettor Education," p. 82.

22. John Stravinsky, "The Highest Rollers," *Golf Magazine,* October 1989, p. 59.

CHAPTER 4: IS THE FIX IN?

1. Art Schlichter with Dick Schaap, "The Self-Destruction of an All-American," *Playboy,* p. 54.

2. Schlichter, "The Self-Destruction of an All-American," p. 136.

3. Schlichter, "The Self-Destruction of an All-American," p. 54.

4. Dave Nightengale, "Baseball's Big-Stakes Game," *The Sporting News,* 1 July 1993, p. 11.

5. Commission on the Review of the National Policy toward Gambling, *Gambling in America* (Washington, D.C.: Government Printing Office), pp. 297–326.

6. Paul Tagliabue, Testimony before House Judiciary Subcommittee on Economic and Commercial Law, 12 September 1991.

7. Bob McCoy, "Amazing Glimpses into Past," *The Sporting News,* 16 October 1989, p. 12.

8. McCoy, "Amazing Glimpses into Past," p. 12.

9. J.M. Fenster, "Nation of Gamblers," *American Heritage,* September 1994, pp. 40–41.

10. Craig Neff, "The Cobb Gambling Scandal," *Sports Illustrated,* 12 June 1989, p. 20.

11. *The Sporting News* editors, "Not-So-Rosy Ordeal Puts Pete Out of Baseball," *The Sporting News,* 22 February 1990, p. 16.

12. *The Sporting News* editors, "Not-So-Rosy Ordeal Puts Pete Out of Baseball," p. 16.

13. George J. Church, "Why Pick on Pete?" *Time,* 10 July 1989, p. 18.

14. Nightengale, "Baseball's Big Stakes Game," p. 9.

15. Nightengale, "Baseball's Big Stakes Game," p. 10.

16. Nightengale, "Baseball's Big Stakes Game," p. 12.

17. Nightengale, "Baseball's Big Stakes Game," p. 11.

18. Richard O'Brien, "The Jordan Affair," *Sports Illustrated,* 16 August 1993, p. 15.

19. *Sports Illustrated* editors, "No Joking Matter," *Sports Illustrated,* 22 January 1990, p. 18.

20. *CQ Researcher,* "When Sports Betting Gets Out of Hand," 18 March 1994, p. 247.

21. Robert Sullivan, "Gambling, Payoffs and Drugs," *Sports Illustrated,* 30 October 1989, p. 40.

22. *Sports Illustrated* editors, "Family Ties," *Sports Illustrated,* 13 November 1989, p. 16.

23. Craig Neff, "A High School Fix?" *Sports Illustrated,* 24 July 1989, p. 11.

24. *Time* editors, "High-Stakes Hoopsters," *Time,* 12 September 1988, p. 33.

25. James Cook, "If Roxborough Says the Spread is 7, It's 7," *Forbes,* 14 September 1992, p. 362.

26. Nightengale, "Baseball's Big-Stakes Game," p. 11.

27. Nightengale, "Baseball's Big Stakes Game," p. 10.

CHAPTER 5: SHOULD ALL BETTING ON SPORTS BE LEGAL?

1. Dave Nightengale, "Baseball's Big-Stakes Game," *The Sporting News,* 1 July 1993, p. 10.

2. George J. Church, "Why Pick on Pete?" *Time,* 10 July 1989, p. 18.

3. Mike Orkin, *Can You Win?* (New York: W.H. Freeman and Company, 1995), pp. 81-82.

4. William Oscar Johnson, "A Sure Bet to Lower Debt," *Sports Illustrated,* 12 September 1991, p. 144.

5. James E. Hosker, Testimony before House Judiciary Subcommittee on Economic and Commercial Law, 12 September 1991.

6. Jerry Adler, Karen Springer and Daniel Glick, "Just Say Yes, Hit Me Again," *Newsweek*, 21 June 1993, p. 68.

7. Johnson, "A Sure Bet to Lower Debt," p. 144.

8. Alexander Wolff, "On Track Betting," *Sports Illustrated*, 20 February 1995, p. 13.

9. Arnold Auerbach, Testimony before House Judiciary Subcommittee on Economic and Commercial Law, 12 September 1991.

10. Nightengale, "Baseball's Big-Stakes Game," p. 11.

11. Nightengale, "Baseball's Big Stakes Game," p. 12.

12. Nightengale, "Baseball's Big Stakes Game," p. 12.

13. James Cook, "If Roxborough Says the Spread is 7, It's 7," *Forbes*, 14 September 1992, p. 350.

14. Cook, "If Roxborough Says the Spread is 7, It's 7," p. 353.

15. Hank Hersch, "Fantasy Busting," *Sports Illustrated*, 9 October 1989, p. 13.

16. James Reston Jr., *Collision at Home Plate* (New York: HarperCollins, 1991), p. 242.

17. Valerie C. Lorenz, Testimony before House Judiciary Subcommittee on Economic and Commercial Law, 12 September 1991.

18. Time editors, "Not For Gamblers," *Time*, 15 June 1992, p. 44.

19. Amy Baratta, "Bid to Legalize Sports Betting in N.J. Fails," *Travel Weekly*, 30 December 1993, p. 21.

20. Cook, "If Roxborough Says the Spread is 7, It's 7," p. 364.

BIBLIOGRAPHY

Abt, Vicki and James F. Smith and Eugene Martin Christiansen. *The Business of Risk, Commercial Gambling in Mainstream America.* Lawrence, Kansas: University Press of Kansas, 1985.

Baratta, Amy. "Bid to Legalize Sports Betting In N.J. Fails." *Travel Weekly,* 30 December 1993.

Bulkeley, William M. and James McNair. "Internet Casinos to Bring Gambling Into the Home." *The San Diego Union-Tribune,* 30 May 1995.

Church, George J. "Why Pick on Pete?" *Time,* 10 July 1989.

Cook, James. "If Roxborough Says the Spread is 7, It's 7." *Forbes,* 14 September 1992.

Crisfield, Deborah. *The Facts About Gambling.* New York: Crestwood House, 1991.

Davis, Bertha. *Gambling in America, A Growth Industry.* New York: Franklin Watts, 1992.

Deford, Frank. "Laying It All on the Line." *Newsweek,* 27 January 1992.

Dolan, Edward F. *Teenagers and Compulsive Gambling.* New York: Franklin Watts, 1994.

Donoghue, Shelagh. "The States Like the Odds." *Time,* 10 July 1989.

Goodman, Robert. *The Luck Business, The Devastating Consequences and Broken Promises of America's Gambling Explosion.* New York: Simon and Schuster, 1995.

Haskins, Jim. Gambling, *Who Really Wins?* New York: Franklin Watts, 1979.

Headline News. Cable News Network, 2 June 1995.

Hersch, Hank. "Fantasy Busting." *Sports Illustrated,* 9 October 1989.

Haubrich-Casperson, Jane and Doug Van Nispen. *Coping With Teen Gambling.* New York: The Rosen Publishing Group, 1993.

Johnson, William Oscar. "A Sure Bet to Lower Debt." *Sports Illustrated,* 2 September 1991.

Layden, Tim. "Bettor Education." *Sports Illustrated,* 3 April 1995.

Layden, Tim. "Book Smart." *Sports Illustrated,* 10 April 1995.

Manteris, Art. *SuperBookie: Inside Las Vegas Sports Gambling.* Chicago, Ill.: Contemporary Books, 1991.

McCoy, Bob, "Amazing Glimpses Into Past." *The Sporting News,* 16 October 1989.

McGarvey, Robert. "Sports Gambling '90s Style." *Sport,* April 1989.

Neff, Craig. "A High School Fix?" *Sports Illustrated,* 24 July 1989.

Neff, Craig. "The Cobb Gambling Scandal." *Sports Illustrated,* 12 June 1989.

Nightengale, Dave. "Baseball's Big-Stakes Game." *The Sporting News,* 1 July 1993.

O'Brien, Richard. "The Jordan Affair." *Sports Illustrated,* 16 August 1993.

Orkin, Mike. *Can You Win?* New York: W.H. Freeman and Company, 1995.

Scarne, John. *Scarne's New Complete Guide to Gambling.* New York: Simon and Schuster, 1986.

Schlichter, Art with Dick Schaap. "The Self-Destruction of an All-American," *Playboy,* February 1984.

Sports Illustrated Editors. "Family Ties." *Sports Illustrated,* 13 November 1989.

Sports Illustrated Editors. "No Joking Matter." *Sports Illustrated,* 22 January 1990.

Stravinsky, John. "The Highest Rollers." *Golf Magazine,* October 1989.

Sullivan, Robert. "Gambling, Payoffs and Drugs." *Sports Illustrated,* 30 October 1989.

The Sporting News Editors. "Not-So-Rosy Ordeal Puts Pete Out of Baseball." *The Sporting News,* 18 February 1990.

Time Editors. "High-Stakes Hoopsters." *Time,* 12 September 1988.

Time Editors. "Not For Gamblers." *Time,* 15 June 1992.

Wagner, Walter. *To Gamble, Or Not To Gamble.* New York: The World Publishing Company, 1972.

Wesch, Hank. "Friday Nights a Smash at Hollywood Park." *The San Diego Union-Tribune,* 26 May, 1995.

Winston, Stuart and Harriet Harris. *Nation of Gamblers, America's Billion-Dollar-A-Day Habit.* Englewood Cliffs, New Jersey: Prentice Hall, Inc., 1984.

Wolff, Alexander. "On Track Betting." *Sports Illustrated,* 20 February 1995.

INDEX

ACKNOWLEDGEMENTS

Photographs are reproduced with the permission of: pp. 2, 10, 26, 30, 40, 70, © James Marshall; p. 6, SportsChrome East/West/Rob Tringali Jr.; p. 9, Little Six Bingo; pp. 14, 23, 24, 36, 38, 49, 74, 94, Independent Photo Service/Nancy Smedstad; pp. 15, 29, 57, CorbisBettmann; p. 16, Independent Photo Service; pp. 17, 18, 19, 51, 56, 58, 59, Archive Photos; pp. 20-21, Columbus Area Chamber of Commerce; p. 28, Gladys Frazier Collection, University of Nevada, Las Vegas Library, Spec. Coll. Neg. #00390006; p. 33, 60, SportsChrome East/West; p. 43, Las Vegas Sports Consultants; p. 52, Sports Illustrated/Walter Iooss; p. 54, People Weekly/Iaro Yamasaki; p. 55, Jeff Topping/Archive Photos; p. 62, Essy Ghavameddini; pp. 63, 76, 77, © Mickey Pfleger; p. 64, Jeff Christensen/Archive Photos; p. 65, SportsChrome East/West/Brian Drake; p. 66, © David Mecey; p. 73, Richard B. Levine; p. 79, Frances M. Roberts; p. 80, Barbara Gauntt; p. 85, Terry Bochatey/Archive Photos.

Charts on pp. 45 and 48 by Cass Brewer. Artwork on pp. 82-83 by John Erste. Cover photograph by © James Marshall.